ZODIAC

CONNECTIONS

ZODIAC
CONNECTIONS

How Your Star Sign Stacks Up

A Book of Astrological Numbers and Lists

ALISE MORALES

ILLUSTRATED BY SHELBY McFADDEN

THUNDER BAY
P·R·E·S·S

San Diego, California

Thunder Bay Press
An imprint of Printers Row Publishing Group
9717 Pacific Heights Blvd, San Diego, CA 92121
www.thunderbaybooks.com • mail@thunderbaybooks.com

Printers Row Publishing Group is a division of Readerlink Distribution Services, LLC.
Thunder Bay Press is a registered trademark of Readerlink Distribution Services, LLC.

Correspondence regarding the content of this book should be sent to Thunder Bay Press, Editorial Department, at the above address. Author, illustration, and rights inquiries should be addressed to Quarto Publishing, The Old Brewery, 6 Blundell St, London, N7 9BH.
www.quarto.com

Thunder Bay Press
Publisher   Peter Norton
Associate Publisher   Ana Parker
Editor   Dan Mansfield

Quarto Publishing
Projects Editor   Anna Galkina
Copyeditor   Julia Shone
Designer   Karin Skånberg
Junior Designer   India Minter
Deputy Art Director   Martina Calvio
Publisher   Lorraine Dickey

Library of Congress Control Number: 2022942534

ISBN: 978-1-6672-0204-4

Printed in China

26 25 24 23 22   1 2 3 4 5

Contents

Meet Alise _____ 6
About This Book_____ 8

Chapter 1
The Star Signs in Lists _____ 10

Aries _____ 12
Taurus _____ 18
Gemini _____ 24
Cancer _____ 30
Leo _____ 36
Virgo _____ 42
Libra _____ 48
Scorpio _____ 54
Sagittarius _____ 60
Capricorn _____ 66
Aquarius _____ 72
Pisces _____ 78

Chapter 2
The Star Signs Compared_____ 84

Friendship _____ 86
Romance _____ 96
In the Workplace _____ 106
Family_____ 116
Travel _____ 124
Lifestyle _____ 132
Fun _____ 140
Health & Wellness _____ 146
Arts & Culture _____ 152

Index _____ 158
Acknowledgments _____ 160

MEET ALISE

The road from comedy writer and actress to amateur astrologer hasn't been the most direct, but I've certainly enjoyed the ride. Like many others in my age group, I started getting interested in astrology several years ago as a diversion from some of the more stressful aspects of my life. Rather than seeing my natal chart, star sign, or horoscope as a prescription to be followed, I've always viewed astrology as an interesting framework through which to view the world. By looking to my star sign (Taurus, by the way) or reviewing my birth chart, I've found that what I'm really thinking about is myself, looking to the future that I'd like to build, and considering values that drive what I do.

Also, it's fun! And I love fun. When I don't have my head in the stars, I'm a writer and comedian based out of Brooklyn, New York, who is best known for my work with Betches Media and my adult puzzle book *I'm a F****** Puzzle Genius* (released in 2020). It was through my work as a writer for various online publications that I first started writing about astrology, publishing horoscopes for a variety of websites, and doing my best to give people accurate astrological information while also making them laugh. With this book, I hope to do the same.

ABOUT THIS BOOK

If you want to take a closer look at a particular sign, whether it's your own or a loved one's, turn to Chapter 1 (pages 10–83). From what to say when they need encouragement to the perfect book to get them for their birthday, you will find inspiration here. Don't forget to look up your rising sign, not just your sun sign. You might find the lists for your rising sign resonating even more!

Chapter 2 (pages 84–157) is where you can turn to compare the signs, with a wealth of fun themes in lists, including Romance (pages 96–105), Family (pages 116–123), Travel (pages 124–131), Health & Wellness (146–151), and much more.

Turn to Chapter 1 (pages 10–83) for in-depth analyses of each sign.

Find all you need to know to compare each sign and how they respond to different situations in the fun lists in Chapter 2 (pages 84–157).

Dip in, dip out, have fun!

THE
STAR SIGNS
IN LISTS

CHAPTER I

ARIES

MODALITY
CARDINAL

RULER PLANE
MARS

SYMBOL

ZODIAC DATES
MARCH 21–APRIL 19

LATIN NAME
ARIES

ENGLISH TRANSLATION
RAM

MOST COMPATIBLE
GEMINI

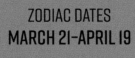

ELEMENT
FIRE

OPPOSITE SIGN
LIBRA

CRYSTAL
RED JASPER

4

THINGS AN ARIES NEVER WANTS TO HEAR

Want to avoid getting burned by an Aries's bad side? That's what we thought. This headstrong sign can be easy to set off if they feel threatened, and they are not afraid to get a little fired up. Avoid the following four phrases unless you think you can take the heat.

1. "CAN YOU TONE IT DOWN?"

2. "WE CAN'T DO IT YOUR WAY."

3. "YOU LOSE."

4. "MEET YOUR NEW BOSS!"

7 SIGNS
AN ARIES IS
flirting
WITH YOU

Think an Aries is flirting with you? Probably. Aries loves the push-and-pull of a good flirtation, and they'll do everything to keep it going for as long as possible. Here are seven signs an Aries has set their sights on you (and they tend to get what they want).

1.
They poke fun at you.

2.
They approach you first.

3.
They argue with you about something silly.

4.
They tell you about their new big idea.

5.
They challenge you to a bet.

6.
They invite you on a last-minute adventure.

7.
You receive mysterious red flowers in the mail.

5 REASONS ARIES MAKE THE **BEST** FRIENDS

If you want a friend who will be loyal until the end, look no further. Passionate Aries will ride hard for you, and will be the first one to stand up if they feel a friend is being disrespected. Here are five reasons an Aries should always be your first phone call after a bad breakup, or if you ever need to go on the run from the law.

1. They're willing to fight for you. Literally.

2. They're forgiving.

3. Their lips are sealed when it comes to secrets.

4. They're always enthusiastic helpers.

5. They keep it real.

10 PLACES AN ARIES SHOULD LIVE, even for just a little while

Competitive Aries looks at life as a game you can win, and that includes traveling the world. They're adventurous and willing to try anything once, especially new cuisine. Here are ten fast-paced cities that Aries should call home, even if it's just for a weekend.

1. Shanghai, China
2. New York, New York
3. Los Angeles, California
4. Tokyo, Japan
5. Marrakech, Morocco
6. Mexico City, Mexico
7. Paris, France
8. Singapore
9. London, England
10. Naples, Italy

5 BOOKS
EVERY
ARIES HAS TO READ
in their lifetime

As the first sign in the zodiac, Aries are leaders. That's why they love to read about leadership—fictional or not. Aries love to come away from a book feeling fired up and motivated, which each of these five books is bound to do.

How to Win Friends and Influence People—Dale Carnegie

The Hunger Games—Suzanne Collins

I Know Why the Caged Bird Sings—Maya Angelou (an Aries!)

The Audacity of Hope—Barack Obama

Dare to Lead—Brené Brown

PERFECT JOBS FOR ARIES

Fiery, self-assured Aries are the people who the concept of "being your own boss" was made for. They're natural-born leaders, so if there's a hierarchy at work they definitely want to be at the top. Aries are ambitious, with high energy and a drive to succeed. Their highly independent career paths will keep Aries motivated without one of those pesky "manager" things other people are always complaining about.

1. CEO
2. *Shark Tank* Judge
3. Emergency First Responder
4. Professional Athlete
5. Film Director
6. Political Fixer
7. Lead Surgeon
8. Tour Guide
9. Real Estate Agent
10. Criminal Mastermind

Affirmations

FOR AN ARIES TO LIVE THEIR BEST LIFE

Passionate, fast-thinking Aries can sometimes find themselves feeling scattered and overwhelmed, and as if they've taken on more than they can handle. These three affirmations will help them reassess and prioritize.

"I am patient."

"I am focused."

"I let go of control."

5
WAYS TO AN ARIES'S
HEART

Confident Aries always has more than their fair share of romantic prospects, meaning you've got to set yourself apart to really grab their attention. Aries loves the thrill of the chase, so if you want to win one's heart, you'd better start running.

1. MENTION YOU'RE CASUALLY SEEING SOMEONE.

2. IGNORE ONE MINUTE, FLIRT THE NEXT.

3. "ACCIDENTALLY" BRUSH HANDS AT THE SNACK TABLE.

4. CHALLENGE THEM TO A BET (AND WIN).

5. EXPRESS REAL INTEREST IN THEIR WORK.

COLORS THAT HELP ARIES
CONNECT
TO THEIR POWER

Aries is a fire sign, meaning they connect most to colors that help their inner flame burn. When they really want to connect to their powers, these six colors can help get them there. Aries in need of a power boost should picture them in their mind's eye.

Burgundy

Orange

Mustard Yellow

Coral

Burnt Sienna

Anything Red

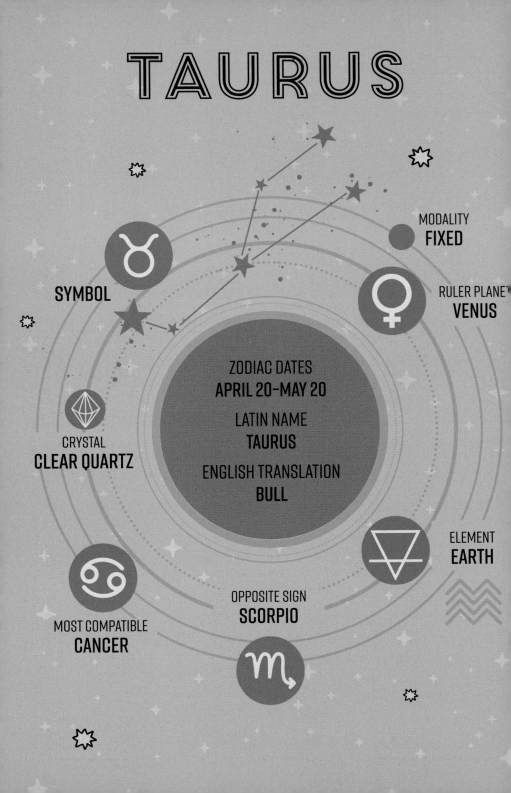

TAURUS

MODALITY
FIXED

SYMBOL

RULER PLANET
VENUS

CRYSTAL
CLEAR QUARTZ

ZODIAC DATES
APRIL 20-MAY 20

LATIN NAME
TAURUS

ENGLISH TRANSLATION
BULL

ELEMENT
EARTH

MOST COMPATIBLE
CANCER

OPPOSITE SIGN
SCORPIO

4 THINGS A TAURUS NEVER WANTS TO HEAR

I think we can all agree it's best to avoid making a bull angry. Stubborn, routine-oriented, and sometimes materialistic, a Taurus can become flustered when things deviate from the norm. Utter any of these four phrases in their vicinity and they'll be seeing red for weeks.

1.
"Your card has been declined."

2.
"We've made some changes to the schedule."

3.
"Out of stock."

4.
"Hurry up."

7 SIGNS A TAURUS IS FLIRTING *with you*

Like anything involving a Taurus, flirting is going to be blink-and-you-miss-it subtle. It's not like a Taurus to cause a big fuss or make a lot of noise to get your attention, and they're not ones to make the first move. With that in mind, these seven subtle flirting techniques are the Taurus equivalent of standing outside your window with a boom box blasting "In Your Eyes" by Peter Gabriel.

1. You notice them staring from across the room.
2. They whisper a joke just for you.
3. They bring you food.
4. They make an excuse to touch you.
5. They offer to build your new bookshelf.
6. You notice them lurking on your social media.
7. They casually drop in a detail from your last conversation (such as your favorite color is taupe, or you broke your toe on a slip-and-slide when you were eight years old).

5 REASONS
TAUREANS MAKE GREAT FRIENDS

Taureans may have some high-maintenance tastes, but they're one of the most low-maintenance and reliable friends you could have. This easygoing sign is never going to be the one in the friendship group who is starting drama, but will be the one with levelheaded advice that ends it all. If your friendship group doesn't have one, fix that ASAP.

1.
They're easygoing.

2.
They'll be your rock in chaotic situations.

3.
They're loyal.

4.
They're not cliquey.

5.
They host the best dinner parties.

10 PLACES
A TAURUS SHOULD LIVE,
even for just a little while

Taureans love nothing more than trying out the foods, sights, and sounds of a new place. The ideal home for a Taurus would be a place that's down-to-earth, but not so remote that you can't pop out for a fancy meal or night on the town. Here are ten cities that fit the bill perfectly:

1. Portland, Oregon	6. Tuscany, Italy
2. Lyon, France	7. Austin, Texas
3. Berlin, Germany	8. Edinburgh, Scotland
4. Copenhagen, Denmark	9. Havana, Cuba
5. Madrid, Spain	10. Prague, Czech Republic

AFFIRMATIONS
FOR A TAURUS TO LIVE THEIR BEST LIFE

Steady Taurus can be easily thrown by changes and unforeseen circumstances. Here are three affirmations for whenever they find their routine interrupted.

"I embrace change."
"I can conquer any challenge."
"I am unafraid to try."

4 WAYS TO A
Taurean's heart

Whoever said the best way to a man's heart is through his stomach was probably talking about a Taurus. Sensual, earthy Taurus loves to feel comfortable and cared for. They connect deeply with physical touch, but won't say no to more material displays of affection either; the shinier, the better.

- TREAT THEM TO A FANCY MEAL.
- TREAT THEM TO A FANCY MEAL YOU COOKED.
- SUGGEST SPENDING THE DAY IN BED.
- WAKE THEM UP WITH A KISS.

COLORS
THAT HELP TAURUS STAY GROUNDED
—

Taurus is the zodiac's first earth sign, so it should come as no surprise that Taureans love to surround themselves with earth tones, particularly greens. These grounding colors help Taureans stay steady and focused in their space, whether they wear them on their person, paint them on the wall, or just keep them in their mind's eye whenever they need to feel a little extra zen.

1. Earth Tones
2. Light Pink
3. Caramel
4. Lavender
5. Sage Green
6. Deep Emerald

5 BOOKS EVERY TAURUS **should read** IN THEIR LIFETIME

Taureans are very sensual, earthy signs, and they want their books to evoke all of that and more. The perfect book for a Taurus is one that is a sensory experience, with prose that feels like a warm blanket. These five books will be the blanket a Taurean needs as they settle in to read, whether it be in bed, the bathtub, or their favorite comfy chair.

1. *The Good Earth*—Pearl S. Buck

2. *One Hundred Years of Solitude*—Gabriel García Márquez

3. *Under the Tuscan Sun*—Frances Mayes

4. *Jane Eyre*—Charlotte Brontë (a Taurus!)

5. *Like Water for Chocolate*—Laura Esquivel

10 PERFECT JOBS FOR TAURUS

Hardworking Taureans love to work with their hands, producing tangible things that people can actually see. They love the work part of work, and wouldn't be satisfied with a job that has them staring at a screen or sitting at a desk all day. The more manual labor, the better.

1. INTERIOR DESIGNER
2. MAKEUP ARTIST
3. GOURMET CHEF
4. FLORIST
5. CARPENTER
6. CONSTRUCTION WORKER
7. LANDSCAPER
8. MASSAGE THERAPIST
9. SOMMELIER
10. MEDIEVAL PEASANT

GEMINI

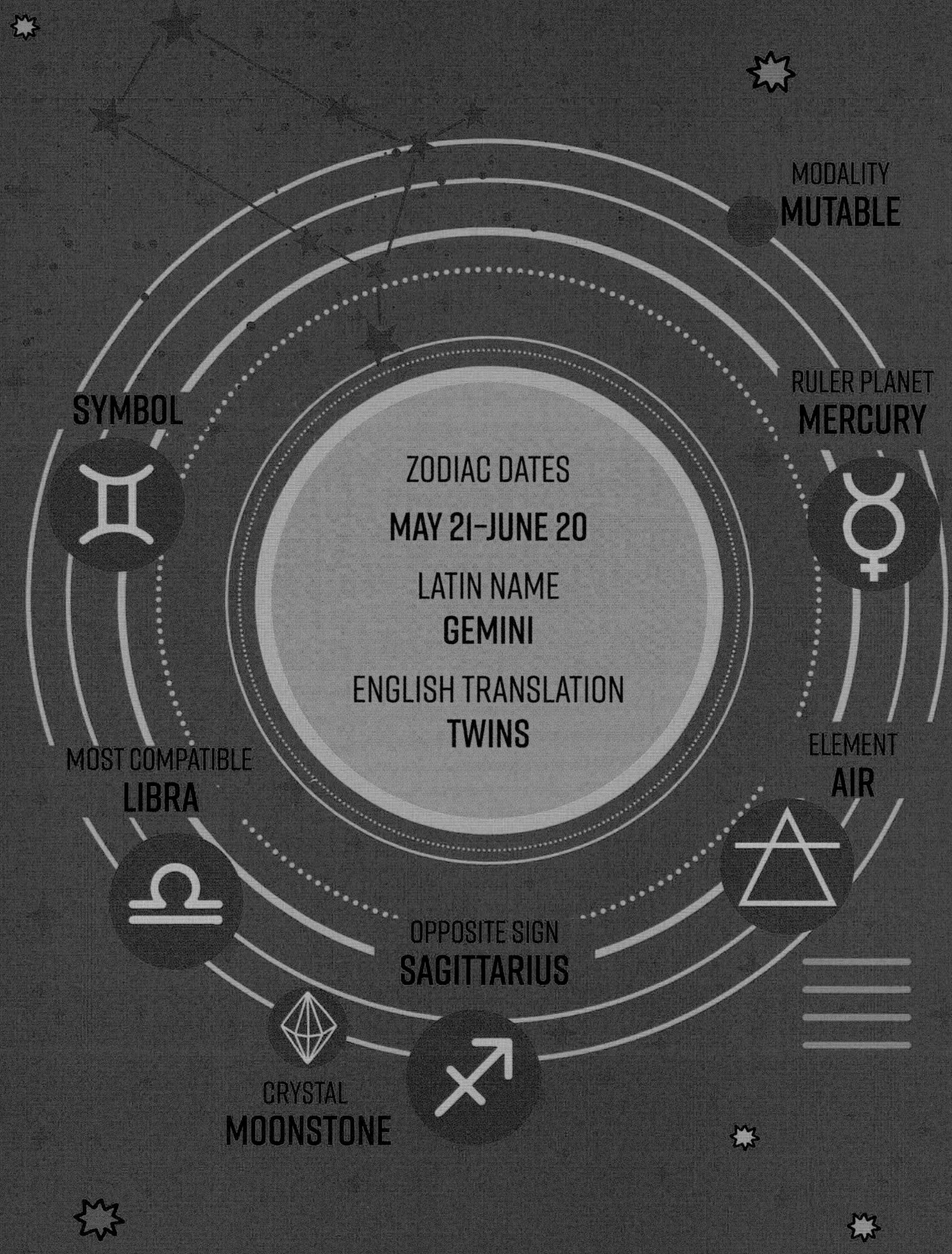

MODALITY
MUTABLE

RULER PLANET
MERCURY

SYMBOL

ZODIAC DATES
MAY 21–JUNE 20

LATIN NAME
GEMINI

ENGLISH TRANSLATION
TWINS

ELEMENT
AIR

MOST COMPATIBLE
LIBRA

OPPOSITE SIGN
SAGITTARIUS

CRYSTAL
MOONSTONE

Sorry, you're not invited.

YOU'VE TOLD ME THIS BEFORE.

We need a firm decision.

4 THINGS A GEMINI NEVER WANTS TO HEAR

Super-social Geminis hate anything that's going to dull their shine or slow their roll. Geminis love flow, and as an air sign they hate to be tied down. Use any of these four phrases around the twins and you can guarantee you won't see them again, no matter which personality they're trying on that day.

WELL, ACTUALLY...

10 PLACES
A GEMINI SHOULD LIVE, EVEN FOR JUST A LITTLE WHILE

Geminis love options, so anywhere they're going to live needs to have a little bit of the best of everything. They want to be intellectually stimulated, with access to museums, art, and, of course, interesting people. Bustling cities with diverse populations are where Geminis will thrive. And it doesn't hurt if they're situated around an elite university or two.

1. REYKJAVÍK, ICELAND
2. OXFORD, ENGLAND
3. CAPE TOWN, SOUTH AFRICA
4. ZURICH, SWITZERLAND
5. HELSINKI, FINLAND
6. SEOUL, SOUTH KOREA
7. AMSTERDAM, NETHERLANDS
8. BOSTON, MASSACHUSETTS
9. PARIS, FRANCE
10. TORONTO, CANADA

6 REASONS *Geminis* ARE THE BEST FRIENDS

Geminis are the fun friend. You can take them anywhere, introduce them to anyone, and they're always going to find a way to get along. Geminis are also connectors, so chances are knowing them means meeting their equally interesting friends, some of whom can become friends of your own. Here are six more reasons you want a Gemini by your side.

1. Your parents will love them.

2. So will your cat.

3. They can always cheer you up with a joke.

4. They have the best fun facts.

5. They're amazing matchmakers.

6. They give great recommendations.

7 SIGNS
A GEMINI IS FLIRTING WITH YOU

Geminis are skilled flirts who are going to do everything in their power to charm the pants off the person they have their eye on. And their power to charm is pretty extensive. If a Gemini flashes a winning smile and engages you in any of these seven activities, it's pretty safe to say they're interested.

1. They leave a funny comment on your latest post. 2. They share a secret.

3. They ask you lots of questions. 4. ...And listen to your answers.

5. They try to hang out (but won't call it a date).

6. They send a funny text. 7. They ask for your opinion.

10 PERFECT JOBS
FOR GEMINI

Geminis need a job that is going to stimulate their mind. Spontaneous, highly social careers that keep them on their toes (and keep their interest) are where they'll excel. Boredom is the death of a Gemini, but any of these ten career paths should keep them engaged and interested.

- Influencer
- Politician
- Magician
- Cult Leader
- Art Teacher

- Public Defender
- Matchmaker
- Romance Novelist
- Flight Attendant
- Hostage Negotiator

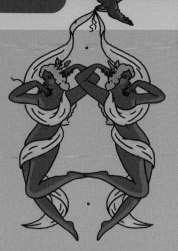

5 WAYS TO A
Gemini's
heart

Geminis love to be surprised and entertained, so unpredictability, intelligence, and wit are your friends. Unfortunately for you, getting a Gemini to fall in love is the easy part—keeping them is a whole other story. These five foolproof ways will help make sure the Gemini in your life sticks around for more than a season.

Send them interesting articles.

•

**Follow that up with
funny memes.**

•

Suggest exciting activities.

•

**Mention your interest in
open relationships.**

•

Disappear for a few days.

•

4 BOOKS
every Gemini has to read in their lifetime

Geminis love two things: to laugh and to think. Books don't need to be laugh-out-loud funny (although it doesn't hurt), but anything that's going to make them crack a smile while also stimulating their mind will make the best addition to a Gemini's already packed bookshelf. Here are four titles they'll be dying to discuss after reading:

Midnight's Children—Salman Rushdie (a Gemini!)

Me Talk Pretty One Day—David Sedaris

Fear and Loathing in Las Vegas—Hunter S. Thompson

Pride and Prejudice—Jane Austen

COLORS THAT HELP GEMINIS THINK
BIG THOUGHTS

Gemini is an air sign, so it's not surprising that their best colors are usually ones you'll see if you look up. Gemini minds are stimulated by light colors that match the light and breezy way they move through life. These six colors provide the perfect backdrop for a Gemini's big thoughts.

- SUNNY YELLOW
- SKY BLUE
- SAGE GREEN
- AQUAMARINE
- SILVER
- MINT

Affirmations
FOR A GEMINI TO LIVE THEIR BEST LIFE

Geminis live with their head in the clouds, meaning sometimes they need affirmations that are going to help tether them back down to earth. While thinking big thoughts is one of a Gemini's superpowers, these affirmations will help them keep a toe on the ground and bring their dreams to reality.

"I am grounded."

"I am calm."

"I have space and time to think."

CANCER

CRYSTAL
LAPIS LAZULI

MODALITY
CARDINAL

RULER PLANE
THE MOON

SYMBOL

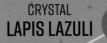

ZODIAC DATES
JUNE 21–JULY 22

LATIN NAME
CANCER

ENGLISH TRANSLATION
CRAB

MOST COMPATIBLE
TAURUS

ELEMENT
WATER

OPPOSITE SIGN
CAPRICORN

4
THINGS A CANCER
NEVER
WANTS TO HEAR

A deeply emotional water sign, Cancers need to have their emotions valued and affirmed. They need validation and companionship from loved ones to survive, so anything that makes them feel isolated or singled out is bound to get a mention in their journal. Avoid these four phrases unless you want a page of your own.

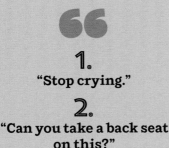

1.
"Stop crying."

2.
"Can you take a back seat on this?"

3.
"Just let it go."

4.
"You're on your own."

6 REASONS CANCERS ARE THE
BEST FRIENDS

Cancers care deeply about the people they love. They're the friend on the camping trip who makes sure everyone has adequate water and is always carrying a first-aid kit, just in case. Think of them as the mother of the zodiac. Here are six reasons why every friendship group needs a Cancer as their group mom.

Their hugs are magic.

They will drop everything to help.

They're always available for a long phone call.

They can tell what's wrong without you having to say.

They love deep conversations.

They give great advice.

10

PLACES A CANCER
should live,
even for just a little while

The concept of "home" is extremely important to a Cancer. They want to live somewhere that values family and friendships. They thrive in places where the population has high emotional intelligence and low levels of workaholism. A Cancer's priorities are their loved ones, and life in any of these ten places will allow them to focus on just that.

➡ BARCELONA, **SPAIN**
➡ DENVER, **COLORADO**
➡ HANOVER, **GERMANY**
➡ MELBOURNE, **AUSTRALIA**
➡ JACÓ, **COSTA RICA**
➡ SIENA, **ITALY**
➡ MADISON, **WISCONSIN**
➡ MONTREAL, **CANADA**
➡ HONOLULU, **HAWAII**
➡ LAKE TAHOE, **CALIFORNIA**

7 SIGNS a Cancer is flirting with you

Cancers are great at keeping their emotions hidden, but that doesn't mean they won't give themselves away when harboring a crush. Loving and maternal, a Cancer flirts by letting you know they care. These seven signs all show a Cancer is thinking of adding you to the family.

1. They blush when you say hello.

2. They offer to help you study.

3. They bring up an inside joke.

4. You notice them making puppy eyes.

5. Their friend tells your friend to tell you they're interested.

6. They offer you half their sandwich.

7. They introduce you to their mom.

AFFIRMATIONS FOR A CANCER TO
live their best life

Cancers can sometimes require lots of external validation to feel good about themselves, but learning to provide that validation from within will help them to truly thrive. Cancers looking to increase their self-esteem should try these three affirmations for letting the love flow from the inside out.

> **"I release what does not serve me."**
> **"I am surrounded by love."**
> **"I am a precious person."**

5 WAYS TO A
Cancer's
HEART

Cancers love love. They feel things deeply, and tend to fall hard, even if they can be rather adept at keeping those feelings hidden. Before letting you in, they want to know they're not going to be burned by someone who doesn't return their feelings. These five moves will help a Cancer feel safe and loved, meaning they'll be yours forever.

♥ Tell them a secret.

♥ Send them a love letter (the longer, the better).

♥ Bring them soup when they're sick.

♥ Send an elaborate birthday present.

♥ Drop them a line, just because.

COLORS
that help Cancers feel their feelings

Cancers need to feel. As a water sign, colors that evoke the deep ocean are ones that will help them to experience emotional release. These six colors will help Cancers let the feelings flow.

♥ BLUE–GRAY
♥ ROYAL BLUE
♥ DEEP PURPLE
♥ SEAFOAM GREEN
♥ EGGSHELL
♥ SILVER

10
perfect jobs
FOR CANCER

Emotional Cancers are going to need a career where their empathy is a strength, and where the occasional at-desk crying session won't result in unemployment. Luckily, these ten career paths all require a Cancer's emotional superpowers rather than trying to repress them.

1. Social Worker
2. Poet
3. School Nurse
4. Dramatic Actor
5. Au Pair
6. Hotelier
7. Antiques Dealer
8. Customer Service Rep
9. Horticulturist
10. Pet Psychic

5 BOOKS
EVERY CANCER
SHOULD READ
IN THEIR LIFETIME

If a Cancer's life has one theme, it's family. Books about the meaning of family that bring on deep emotions will be the ones to grab a Cancer's heart, and they're definitely not afraid of a good cry. Any of these five books will give Cancers the emotional release they need, whether it be sadness or joy, or a mixture of both.

Is Everyone Hanging Out Without Me?
(And Other Concerns)
Mindy Kaling (a Cancer!)

A Little Life
Hanya Yanagihara

Beloved
Toni Morrison

The Year of Magical Thinking
Joan Didion

The Grapes of Wrath
John Steinbeck

LEO

CRYSTAL
CARNELIAN

MODALITY
FIXED

RULER PLANET
THE SUN

ZODIAC DATES

JULY 23–AUGUST 22

LATIN NAME

LEO

ENGLISH TRANSLATION

LION

SYMBOL

ELEMENT
FIRE

MOST COMPATIBLE
LIBRA

OPPOSITE SIGN
AQUARIUS

5
REASONS
LEOS ARE THE BEST FRIENDS EVER

Despite having a reputation for being a little self-centered, Leos bond for life. They want their friends to shine alongside them, and love nothing more than using little tokens to show they care. They're always happy to get the party started with a group text suggesting weekend plans. Here are just five reasons fun-loving Leos are some of the best friends anyone can have.

★ **They give the best gifts.**

★ **And the best compliments.**

★ **They always respond to texts.**

★ **They keep things interesting.**

★ **They always have your back.**

7 SIGNS A LEO IS Flirting WITH YOU

Leos are some of the most natural flirts in the zodiac, so don't be surprised when one puts the moves on you. Here are seven surefire ways to know that a Leo is interested.

1.
They say "I am flirting with you."

2.
They make a raunchy joke.

3.
A wink from across the room.

4.
They get a little jealous.

5.
They bring you a drink from the bar.

6.
They invite you out on the town.

7.
They compliment your style.

10 PLACES

A LEO SHOULD LIVE, EVEN FOR JUST A LITTLE WHILE

As the most fashionable zodiac sign, it's no surprise that Leos thrive in some of the world's most fashionable cities. Here are ten places a Leo should call home, even if it's just for a few days.

LEOS DAZZLE LIKE THE SUN

- ➡ **LOS ANGELES,** CALIFORNIA
- ➡ **NEW YORK,** NEW YORK
- ➡ **LONDON,** ENGLAND
- ➡ **PARIS,** FRANCE
- ➡ **MILAN,** ITALY
- ➡ **TOKYO,** JAPAN
- ➡ **VIENNA,** AUSTRIA
- ➡ **ROME,** ITALY
- ➡ **SINGAPORE**
- ➡ **SHANGHAI,** CHINA

4 THINGS A LEO NEVER WANTS TO HEAR

Want to get under a Leo's skin? Utter any of these four phrases and you are bound to get on the lion's bad side. BE WARNED.

1. "YOU'VE GOT SOMETHING IN YOUR TEETH."

2. "THIS ISN'T ALL ABOUT YOU."

3. "SORRY, I FORGOT YOUR NAME."

4. "LET'S KEEP IT LOW-KEY TONIGHT."

10 PERFECT jobs for Leo

Leos love the spotlight. That means they're not ones to take a back seat to anyone and prefer to be the star of the show. Jobs where they get to lead and be seen are going to be the ones that keep Leos happiest. These ten jobs will be sure to help the lion stay motivated (and achieve their ultimate goal of being the coolest person at their high school reunion).

1. CELEBRITY STYLIST
2. PR GURU
3. LOUNGE SINGER
4. MOTIVATIONAL SPEAKER
5. WEDDING PLANNER
6. CAMPAIGN MANAGER
7. CIRCUS PERFORMER
8. BROADWAY STAR
9. FASHION BLOGGER
10. ENTREPRENEUR

AFFIRMATIONS FOR A LEO
to live their *BEST* life

While Leos exude confidence, life in the public eye means they can sometimes get caught up in trying to be perfect for others. These three affirmations will help Leos keep in mind that it's what's inside that really counts.

"MY INNER BEAUTY MAKES ME STRONG."

"I RELEASE MYSELF FROM JUDGMENT."

"I EMBRACE MY FLAWS."

COLORS
THAT HELP LEOS SHINE BRIGHT
like a diamond

Leos love to be bold, and their power colors reflect that. Leos run hot, and tend toward warm colors with rich, full undertones. Colors that reflect the Sun (Leo's ruler) will help lions take their place as king of the jungle.

Gold

Orange

Deep Purple

Blood Red

Burnt Orange

Kumquat

5 BOOKS
EVERY LEO HAS TO READ
in their lifetime

Looking for the next book to add to a Leo's collection? Glitz- and glamour-loving Leos want to be transported into the lives of the rich and famous, with particular attention paid to descriptions of clothes and style. Here are five books that Leo will both love to read and use as style inspo for years to come.

The Great Gatsby
F. Scott Fitzgerald

The Age of Innocence
Edith Wharton

Crazy Rich Asians
Kevin Kwan

Wuthering Heights
Emily Brontë

The Devil Wears Prada
Lauren Weisberger

5 WAYS
TO A LEO'S
HEART

Want to woo the Leo in your life? Get in line. Leos naturally have tons of admirers, but don't worry! Here are five guaranteed ways to win their heart. And remember, when Leo is involved, flattery is everything.

1. SUBTLE FLIRTING.

2. COMPLIMENT THEIR OUTFIT.

3. BE FUN AT PARTIES.

4. DON'T GET TOO LOVEY-DOVEY.

5. DRESS UP FOR YOUR DATES.

VIRGO

CRYSTAL
TIGER'S EYE

MODALITY
MUTABLE

SYMBOL

ZODIAC DATES
AUGUST 23–SEPTEMBER 22

LATIN NAME
VIRGO

ENGLISH TRANSLATION
VIRGIN

RULER PLANET
MERCURY

MOST COMPATIBLE
CAPRICORN

ELEMENT
EARTH

OPPOSITE SIGN
PISCES

10 PLACES

VIRGOS SHOULD LIVE, EVEN FOR JUST A LITTLE WHILE

Virgos love order, meaning they enjoy living in well-kept cities and towns that were designed with purpose. Nothing makes them happier than explaining their city's transit map to a visiting guest. And is it any surprise that these ten places also happen to be some of the cleanest and most well-planned cities in the world? I don't think so.

1.	Sapporo, Japan	6.	Paris, France
2.	Brisbane, Australia	7.	Washington, D.C.
3.	Calgary, Canada	8.	Seoul, South Korea
4.	Tallinn, Estonia	9.	Wellington, New Zealand
5.	Chandigarh, India	10.	Stockholm, Sweden

4 THINGS A VIRGO
NEVER
wants to hear

Virgos are reserved, but they are also perfectionists. They like things to be done, and done right. Consummate supervisors, they keep an eye on everything and get frustrated when things are done wrong, or simply not in the way they would like. If you want to avoid getting on their bad side, don't let them hear any of these four sentences come out of your mouth.

"IT'S GOOD ENOUGH."

"SPEECH! SPEECH! SPEECH!"

"I DON'T NEED YOUR HELP."

"SORRY FOR THE MESS!"

7 SIGNS
A VIRGO IS
flirting with you

Virgos are not one of those signs that rush into love (hi, Pisces), so chances are it may take some time for them to turn on the charm. Once they do, their drive to be useful means that you can expect a helping hand to start popping up wherever you need it, whether it be help assembling your new IKEA furniture or working through a complicated calculus equation—even if it means teaching themselves how to do calculus first.

1. THEY SEND YOU SOMETHING, JUST BECAUSE.
2. THEY HELP CLEAN UP YOUR BIRTHDAY PARTY.
3. THEY ACTUALLY PLAN YOUR BIRTHDAY PARTY.
4. THEY LAUGH EXTRA LOUD AT YOUR JOKES.
5. THEY LOCK EYES WITH YOU WHILE TALKING.
6. THEY TALK ABOUT THE FUTURE (AND INCLUDE YOU IN IT).
7. THEY LEAN IN CLOSE.

COLORS
THAT HELP VIRGOS
FOCUS

Virgos' best colors are ones that are going to help them focus their minds. As an earth sign, they're going to be looking for colors found in nature, particularly ones that remind them of fruits and berries. Here are six that are bound to help them settle the mind and get focused on the task at hand.

Peach
Mauve
Cherry Red
Moss Green
Tree Bark
Purple Grape

AFFIRMATIONS FOR A VIRGO
to live their best life

Rigid Virgos can sometimes let themselves get stuck in their ways, allowing themselves to become bogged down with judgments of themselves and others. While their drive to get things right is what fuels them to succeed, these three affirmations will help release them from the perfectionism that can wreck a Virgo's self-worth.

"I open my mind to new possibilities."
"I release all judgment of others."
"I am perfectly imperfect."

5 BOOKS
A VIRGO HAS TO READ *in their lifetime*

Intelligent, organized Virgos want books that are going to challenge their brains and celebrate the power of the mind. They love books with a purpose and that feel like an accomplishment to complete, whether it be due to content or sheer size. Here are five books a Virgo would be proud to add to their alphabetized bookshelf.

1. *The 7 Habits of Highly Effective People*—**Stephen R. Covey**
2. *Outliers: The Story of Success*—**Malcolm Gladwell**
3. *The Life-Changing Magic of Tidying Up*—**Marie Kondo**
4. *Matilda*—**Roald Dahl (a Virgo!)**
5. *Infinite Jest*—**David Foster Wallace**

5 WAYS TO A VIRGO'S
Heart

Earthy Virgo is not superficial, so putting on your cutest outfit isn't going to work here. Instead, focus on showing a Virgo that you're a smart, capable individual with good hygiene and a stable bank account. They love to be useful, so letting them help you while also displaying your own strengths is the best way to get a Virgo to add saying "I do" to their to-do list.

1. Let them help you with something.
2. Compliment something small in their home—such as the way they've organized their bookshelf or how clean the doorknobs are.
3. Take it slow.
4. Tell them your five-year plan.
5. Smell like fresh laundry.

♍

5 Reasons Virgos Are the *Best Friends* Ever

Virgos keep their circle small, meaning they really have time to devote to their friendships. These ultra-reliable earth signs will be there when you need them. They value honesty, and their friends know they can trust they're getting a Virgo's true opinion. Yes, sometimes that opinion can be a little critical, but here are just five reasons why a Virgo's critical eye is a price worth paying for their friendship.

1. THEY'LL LET YOU COPY THEIR HOMEWORK.

2. THEY'LL THINK THINGS THROUGH (EVEN WHEN YOU DON'T).

3. THEY'LL ALWAYS BE HONEST WITH YOU.

4. THEY'RE GREAT PROBLEM-SOLVERS.

5. THEY'RE LOYAL UNTIL THE END.

10 PERFECT JOBS FOR VIRGO

Perfectionism is a Virgo's curse, but it's also their superpower. When it comes to careers, Virgos are going to want to choose a field where getting it right is part of the job, and where less than 100 percent is not accepted. Virgos love rising to high expectations, and want a career that will challenge them to deliver on a high level again and again. Luckily for them, here are ten jobs that will challenge them every day.

1.	Police Chief
2.	Executive Assistant
3.	Magazine Editor
4.	Detective
5.	Librarian
6.	Veterinarian
7.	Nutritionist
8.	Life Coach
9.	Accountant
10.	Computer Engineer

LIBRA

MODALITY
CARDINAL

RULER PLANET
VENUS

SYMBOL

ZODIAC DATES
SEPTEMBER 23–OCTOBER 22

LATIN NAME
LIBRA

ENGLISH TRANSLATION
BALANCE

MOST COMPATIBLE
GEMINI

ELEMENT
AIR

OPPOSITE SIGN
ARIES

CRYSTAL
ROSE QUARTZ

4 THINGS
A LIBRA
NEVER
WANTS TO HEAR

Social, indecisive Libras are introverted extroverts. They love to be among friends, but can find themselves feeling trapped or backed into a corner when put on the spot. These egalitarians hate choosing sides, and will harbor a grudge against someone who makes things unpleasant or awkward. Luckily, staying on a Libra's good side is fairly easy—just avoid these four phrases:

"Time to decide."
"You're the first one here!"
"Pick a side."
"I heard a rumor about you..."

10 PERFECT JOBS FOR LIBRA

Libras are represented by a set of scales, and their quest for balance and justice should be central to any career they take on. They love to bring people and things together, and their love of beauty is always at the forefront of their minds. These ten careers will help them play to those strengths.

1. UN Ambassador
2. Judge
3. Art Dealer
4. Art Thief
5. Fashion Buyer
6. Interior Designer
7. Talent Agent
8. Con Artist
9. Personal Stylist
10. Luxury Car Dealer

7 SIGNS A LIBRA IS
FLIRTING WITH YOU

Thanks to their easy manner, Libras are natural flirts. But their indecisive nature means you might have to be on the lookout for cues to make the first move. If you get the feeling a Libra is debating whether or not to ask you out, they probably are. These seven signs may also provide clues.

1. THEY MATCH YOU ON A DATING APP "AS A JOKE."
2. THEY ADD YOU TO THE GROUP CHAT.
3. THEY HINT AT BEING FREE NEXT WEEKEND.
4. THEY GRAB YOU SOMETHING OFF THE TOP SHELF.
5. THEY PERSONALLY INVITE YOU TO THEIR BIRTHDAY PARTY.
6. THEY'RE ALWAYS THE FIRST TO "LIKE" YOUR SELFIES.
7. THEY USE A HEART EMOJI IN EVERY TEXT.

10 PLACES A LIBRA SHOULD LIVE, even for just a little while

Libras are the friendliest sign in the zodiac, meaning they will be the most comfortable living in some of the world's friendliest places. These locations are known for their hospitality, making them the perfect place for a Libra to settle (until they change their mind and decide it's time to go somewhere else).

1. MÁLAGA, SPAIN
2. MANCHESTER, ENGLAND
3. CHARLESTON, SOUTH CAROLINA
4. GLASGOW, SCOTLAND
5. LISBON, PORTUGAL
6. SAN JOSÉ, COSTA RICA
7. MUSCAT, OMAN
8. MONTREÁL, CANADA
9. STONETOWN, ZANZIBAR
10. DUBAI, UNITED ARAB EMIRATES

AFFIRMATIONS FOR A LIBRA
TO LIVE THEIR BEST LIFE

Indecisive Libras can find themselves under a lot of stress when it comes time to choose. Learning to handle life's inevitable decisions will help keep Libras happy, and make their sense of justice even stronger. These three affirmations will help with that journey.

"My intuition is strong."
"I connect to my sense of justice."
"I have the power to make sound choices."

5 WAYS
to a Libra's heart

Lovely Libras love pretty things, meaning their eyes are the keys to their hearts. That's not to say they are superficial—Libras can find beauty in all things. Woo a Libra by presenting them with beauty, such as a night of music, a picnic in the park, or any of these five ideas for getting their heart pumping.

♥ Tell them they're beautiful.
♥ Take them to an art museum.
♥ Emphasize your similarities.
♥ Bring them something shiny.
♥ Smile often.

Colors
THAT HELP LIBRAS
SEE BEAUTY ALL AROUND THEM

Libras are light and friendly people, and they enjoy light and friendly colors. They like colors that feel warm and happy, and that have a light touch (in case they want to paint over them again tomorrow). Pick a flower in any of these six colors and present it to a Libra. They'll be beaming for days to come.

Bubblegum Pink
Cream
Mint Green
Teal
Lavender
Champagne

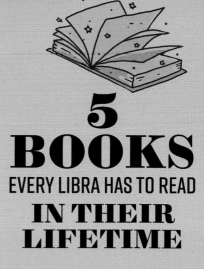

5 REASONS LIBRAS ARE THE *best friends ever*

Libras are good people and great friends. Their obsession with reason means they'll always give you level-headed counsel. They specialize in compromise, and any friendship group would benefit from having a Libra at the table— especially when things get a little too heated at brunch. Here are five other ways that Libras make the best brunch companions.

1. They're easy to talk to.
2. You can take them anywhere and introduce them to anyone.
3. They're great listeners.
4. They're even better advice-givers.
5. They genuinely care.

5 BOOKS
EVERY LIBRA HAS TO READ
IN THEIR LIFETIME

Have we mentioned that Libras love beautiful things? Well, they do. They love lyrical prose that evokes beautiful imagery, and want books that will transport them somewhere else. Books that explore the nature of beauty itself or of justice, fairness, and equality (like the five below) will also keep a Libra turning the pages.

1. *The White Album*—Joan Didion
2. *Their Eyes Were Watching God*— Zora Neale Hurston
3. *The Picture of Dorian Gray*— Oscar Wilde (a Libra!)
4. *The Kite Runner*—Khaled Hosseini
5. *Madame Bovary*—Gustave Flaubert

SCORPIO

MODALITY
FIXED

RULER PLANET
VENUS

CRYSTAL
CITRINE

ZODIAC DATES
OCTOBER 23–NOVEMBER 21

LATIN NAME
SCORPIO

ENGLISH TRANSLATION
SCORPION

SYMBOL

ELEMENT
WATER

OPPOSITE SIGN
TAURUS

MOST COMPATIBLE
PISCES

5

REASONS SCORPIOS
ARE THE BEST FRIENDS EVER

Scorpios are deep, and so are their friendships. Surface-level relationships are not interesting to a Scorpio, who prefers the pressure of the ocean's deepest depths. When a Scorpio calls you a friend, they're willing to go there with you, whether it means holding your hand through a breakup or while jumping out of your first plane. Here are five reasons it's great to know a Scorpio who's got your back.

1. THEY ARE DEEPLY COMPASSIONATE.
2. YOU CAN TRUST THEM WITH ANYTHING.
3. THEY WON'T LIE.
4. THEY'RE OPEN AND HONEST.
5. YOU NEVER HAVE TO TRY TO IMPRESS THEM.

10
PERFECT
JOBS FOR SCORPIO

A Scorpio is only happy if they're unlocking the mysteries of life, exploring taboos, and opening doors that society tells you are supposed to stay shut. They love to make their own way, and don't care if what they're doing is considered acceptable or a "real job" by society at large. Here are ten careers that will satisfy a Scorpio's thirst for the unknown.

Cold Case Investigator

International Super Spy

Forensic Psychologist

Psychic

Sex Therapist

Mortician

Pirate

Mystery Novelist

Ghost Hunter

Rock Star

AFFIRMATIONS
for a Scorpio to live their best life

Scorpios can often be misunderstood, which can make them feel isolated and alone. Add that to a fear of vulnerability and they can end up feeling quite isolated. These three affirmations will help remind even the most solo of Scorpios that they're not alone.

"I am loved."

———

"I connect to those around me."

———

"My emotions are my strength."

5 BOOKS A SCORPIO
has to read in their lifetime

Scorpios want to have their minds blown. They love to explore the world's dark side. They're not afraid to ask life's most perplexing questions or to look at the underbelly of society. These five books are filled with these examinations, and will help a Scorpio on their quest to figure out what fuels society's darkest impulses.

A Clockwork Orange
Anthony Burgess

Brave New World
Aldous Huxley

Lolita
Vladimir Nabokov

Kindred
Octavia E. Butler

Do Androids Dream of Electric Sheep?
Philip K. Dick

COLORS THAT HELP SCORPIOS
GO DEEP

Scorpios love dark spaces that reflect the darkness within. That's not to say they want things to be sad or scary, but they prefer the calm that darker colors bring. When trying to go deep, say for a creative project or difficult conversation, Scorpios should conjure one of these six colors to connect to the depth within.

⇨Maroon ⇨Blood Red

⇨Burgundy ⇨Cyan

⇨Deep Purple ⇨Black

5
WAYS TO A *SCORPIO'S HEART*

Scorpios are attracted to darkness, so the more mysterious you can make yourself, the better. They are the epitome of people who "always" fall for the bad guy and like their romantic relationships to come with a hint of danger. Don't share everything about yourself right away, but rather share tantalizing nuggets of info at each encounter. Pair that with these five flirtation techniques, and even darkness-loving Scorpio will want to stick around into the daytime.

1. Wear a leather jacket.

2. Make them a moody playlist.

3. Hint at a deep, dark secret.

4. Never, ever be fake.

5. Surprise them.

10 PLACES A SCORPIO SHOULD LIVE,
even for just a little while

Scorpios are nightlife personified, meaning they're most attracted to places that truly come alive after dark. Not knowing the language or having major cultural barriers doesn't scare them. Scorpios aren't afraid to immerse themselves in a new culture and just figure it out. Here are ten places a Scorpio should drop themselves off to figure it out ASAP.

- ›››› Miami, **Florida**
- ›››› Tokyo, **Japan**
- ›››› New Orleans, **Louisiana**
- ›››› Rio de Janeiro, **Brazil**
- ›››› Buenos Aires, **Argentina**
- ›››› Bangkok, **Thailand**
- ›››› Mykonos, **Greece**
- ›››› Belgrade, **Serbia**
- ›››› Bali, **Indonesia**
- ›››› Ibiza, **Spain**

7 SIGNS
a Scorpio is
flirting
WITH YOU

Chances are you'll know a Scorpio is flirting with you, as they like to come on hot and heavy. That said, their mysterious nature can leave you thinking, "Are they joking, or are they seriously interested?" The answer is both. Mercurial Scorpio isn't going to tell you their feelings at first blush. But stick around long enough and they'll make the first move, probably in one of these seven forms.

1. They ask you to marry them. As a "joke."
2. They kiss your hand. (Also "a joke.")
3. They make deep eye contact.
4. They talk to you all night.
5. They slip you their number.
6. They send long, thoughtful texts.
7. You catch them leaning in for a kiss.

4
things a Scorpio **never** wants to hear

Intense and deeply mysterious, Scorpios love bringing secrets to light...unless we're talking about their own. Scorpios can be hard to read, and it can only take a second before they unleash their poison sting. Leave these sentences at the door unless you want to get hit.

"That's personal."

"You can't go in there."

"I can't tell if you're joking."

"I know your secret."

SAGITTARIUS

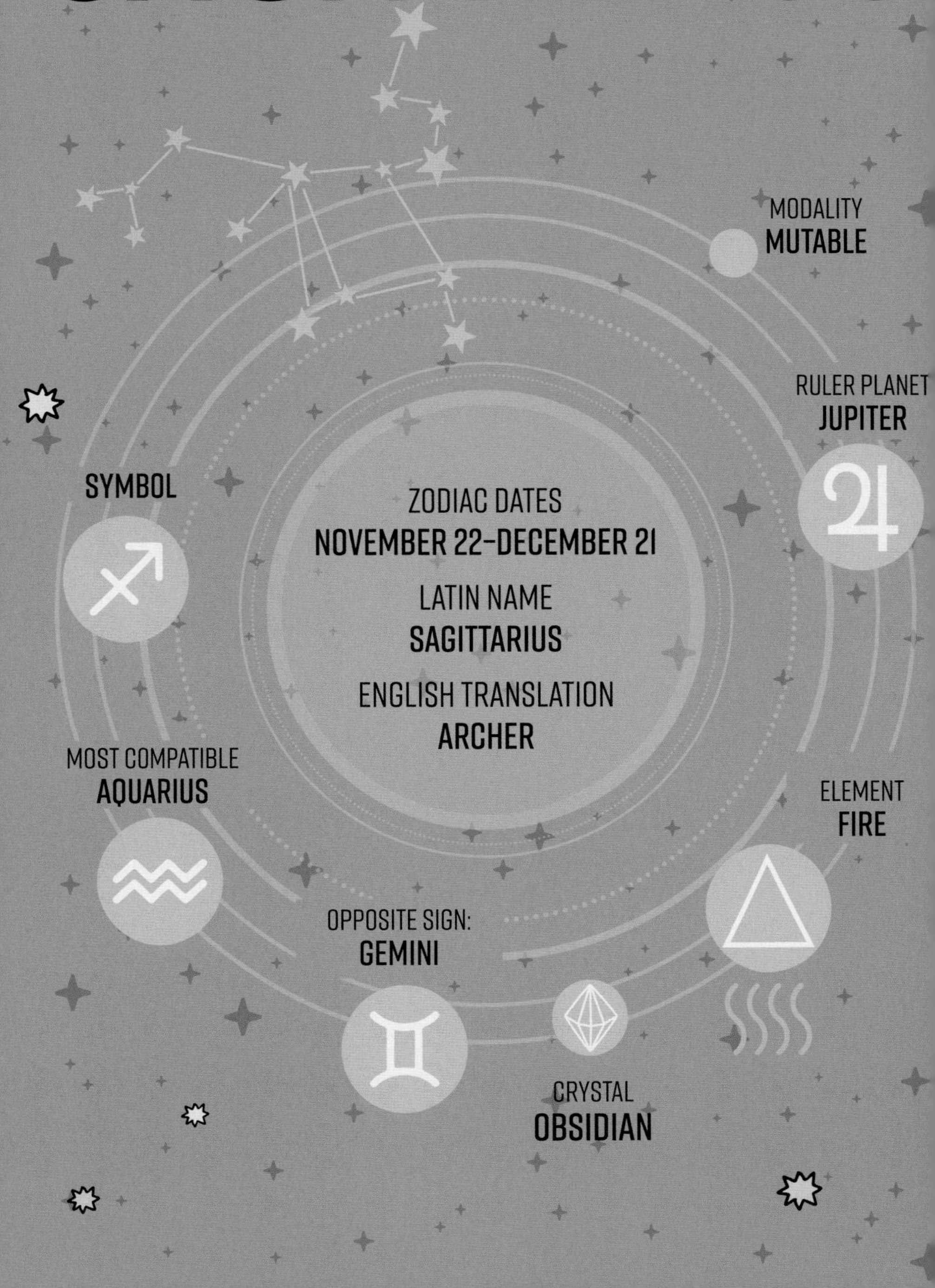

MODALITY
MUTABLE

RULER PLANET
JUPITER

♃

SYMBOL

↗

ZODIAC DATES
NOVEMBER 22–DECEMBER 21

LATIN NAME
SAGITTARIUS

ENGLISH TRANSLATION
ARCHER

MOST COMPATIBLE
AQUARIUS

ELEMENT
FIRE

OPPOSITE SIGN:
GEMINI

CRYSTAL
OBSIDIAN

10 PERFECT JOBS FOR SAGITTARIUS

Let's face it, "job" and "Sagittarius" are not natural fits. That's not to say that they're not hardworking, they're just not ones to be told what to do or where to be. And don't even get them started about requesting vacation time. These ten jobs will play to a Sagittarian's strengths, meaning they'll never feel like they're working and won't find themselves running for the hills.

1. PARTY PLANNER
2. CRUISE DIRECTOR
3. TRAVEL AGENT
4. VIDEO GAME DESIGNER
5. PROFESSOR OF EVERYTHING
6. ADVICE COLUMNIST
7. FLIGHT ATTENDANT
8. SPIRIT GUIDE
9. TRAVEL WRITER
10. BIG RIG TRUCKER

Affirmations
for a Sagittarian to live their best life

For a Sagittarian, their freedom is their greatest asset. It is their job to protect it at all costs. When a Sagittarian feels their wings being clipped, or their freedom being challenged, one of these three affirmations will help them breathe freely once more.

"I am free."

"I see abundance all around me."

"I protect my independence."

COLORS
THAT HELP A SAGITTARIAN
ACHIEVE ENLIGHTENMENT

Sagittarians are truth seekers. They like bright, powerful colors that remind them of their bright, powerful brains. They love colors that will evoke their travels (or imagined travels), and prefer hot, flavorful hues to anything muted or dull. Sagittarians can incorporate any of these into their wardrobe when they want to feel their highest selves.

HOT PINK · DEEP PURPLE
FIRE ENGINE RED · EMERALD GREEN
SAFFRON · AMBER

5 reasons Sagittarius is the best friend EVER

Have we mentioned that Sagittarians are fun? Hang around one, and you're bound to have a good time. Archers are great friends because they're so delightful to be around, and because you can always count on them to be up on the latest tunes and trends. These thoughtful free spirits make great companions, particularly for these five reasons.

1. They're the life of the party.

2. They've got the best stories.

3. They give great pep talks.

4. They can always make you laugh.

5. Their energy is infectious.

10 PLACES

SAGITTARIUS SHOULD LIVE,
even for just a little while

There's nothing a Sagittarian loves more than to travel. As natural wanderers, archers want to experience all the world has to offer from the highest highs to the lowest lows (literally: their bucket list includes Mount Everest). These ten destinations will help quench a Sagittarian's wanderlust—for a time. Then they'll pack a bag and move on to the next ten, and the next ten, and the next...

Sedona, **Arizona**

Paris, **France**

Uluru, **Australia**

Rishikesh, **India**

Machu Picchu, **Peru**

Cairo, **Egypt**

Kathmandu, **Nepal**

Fairbanks, **Alaska**

Hamburg, **Germany**

Marrakech, **Morocco**

5 WAYS TO A SAGITTARIAN'S HEART

Restless Sagittarians love to be kept on their toes. They believe that variety is the spice of life, and want to be surprised, titillated, and a little frustrated by their partner. They'll need someone who's going to embrace their free spirit, and by making these five moves you'll definitely show them you can.

- ♥ Debate with them.

- ♥ Give them a killer book recommendation.

- ♥ Take them on a surprise vacation.

- ♥ Spend a night out on the town.

- ♥ Tell them exactly how you feel.

5 BOOKS EVERY SAGITTARIAN HAS TO READ IN THEIR LIFETIME

Sagittarians want books that will do two things: satisfy their wanderlust and give them a dose of philosophy. They want books that will give them an opportunity to contemplate the big questions, particularly while imagining exotic adventures in far-off lands. Here are five books to help a Sagittarian get transported to another world.

1.
Zen and the Art of Motorcycle Maintenance
ROBERT M. PIRSIG

2.
Wild
CHERYL STRAYED

3.
Siddhartha
HERMANN HESSE

4.
The Alchemist
PAULO COELHO

5.
The Complete Poems
OF EMILY DICKINSON
(a Sagittarius!)

7

SIGNS
a Sagittarian
is flirting with you

Sagittarians live with their hearts wide open, meaning they are not afraid to fall in love. And fall in love. And fall in love. If you happen to catch one's eye, they'll do their best to make you laugh and show you they're the life of the party. They love fun, and by bringing you in on it, they're showing you they'd like to keep you around.

1. THEY WRITE YOU A LOVE SONG (HELLO, TAYLOR SWIFT).
2. THEY WHISK YOU AWAY ON AN IMPROMPTU ADVENTURE.
3. THEY SHOW UP UNANNOUNCED.
4. THEY LET YOU BORROW THEIR FAVORITE BOOK.
5. THEY GIVE YOU A PEP TALK.
6. THEY TRY TO MAKE YOU LAUGH.
7. THEY PLAYFULLY PUSH YOUR BUTTONS.

3 THINGS SAGITTARIUS NEVER WANTS TO HEAR

Loud, boisterous Sagittarius doesn't like anything that will stop the party. They value honesty above all things and will be the first to call out liars and fakes. Unless you want to get pierced by the archer's arrow, you'd do best to avoid saying these four sentences.

"Can you lower your voice?"

"Let's focus on one thing."

"You have the wrong info."

"I lied."

CAPRICORN

MODALITY
CARDINAL

SYMBOL

RULER PLANE
SATURN

ZODIAC DATES
DECEMBER 22–JANUARY 19

LATIN NAME
CAPRICORN

ENGLISH TRANSLATION
SEA GOAT

MOST COMPATIBLE
VIRGO

ELEMENT
EARTH

OPPOSITE SIGN
CANCER

CRYSTAL
MALACHITE

10 PLACES
A CAPRICORN SHOULD LIVE, EVEN FOR JUST A LITTLE WHILE

Capricorns don't need a lot to be happy—just a quiet place where they can connect to nature and not have their routine disturbed. These ten peaceful destinations have some of the most beautiful, natural vistas in the world, perfect for relaxing with a cup of tea after a long day of work (aka a Capricorn's happy place).

1. Boulder, Colorado
2. Cuzco, Peru
3. Ambergris Caye, Belize
4. Zion, Utah
5. Devon, England
6. Skåne, Sweden
7. Vancouver, Canada
8. Tasmania, Australia
9. Big Sur, California
10. Bergen, Norway

5 WAYS
to a Capricorn's heart

Capricorns are serious people. They want to see an investment from you before they open up, and are absolutely willing to wait until they feel sure their standards have been met. That said, Capricorns love family, and once they decide to let you into theirs, their warmth radiates from the inside out.

♥

Be on time (aka early).

♥

Have clean fingernails.

♥

Focus on the friendship.

♥

Tell them about your family.

♥

Show them your cutest baby pictures.

5 REASONS CAPRICORNS ARE THE BEST FRIENDS EVER

Under a Capricorn's rock-solid work ethic is a tender heart and one of the best friends you could ask for. They are loyal to a fault, and you can always count on them to do what they say they're going to do. They're the friend who shows up on time, with extra toothbrushes in case someone forgot. And here are five more reasons they make incredible friends.

1. They never forget a birthday.

2. They want to see you succeed (and will help you get there).

3. They keep their cool in stressful situations.

4. They'll always let you vent.

5. Their friendship is lifelong.

7 SIGNS
a Capricorn is flirting with you

Capricorns are good at hiding their emotions, so figuring out their feelings will mean you need to keep an eye on body language. Once it's time, they'll be direct. They don't like to waste a lot of time on someone who isn't interested, and will want to get plans on the books right away. Here are seven signs you should expect a calendar invite asking you to dinner any day now.

–

They text back during working hours.

–

They suggest hanging out "as friends."

–

They crack a smile.

–

They always greet you with a hug.

–

They tell a corny joke.

–

They bring flowers.

–

They make a pros and cons list for asking you out.

AFFIRMATIONS FOR A CAPRICORN TO
LIVE THEIR BEST LIFE

If you've gotten the sense that Capricorns can sometimes push themselves to work too hard, you're right. While a strong work ethic is a good thing, these three affirmations will help Capricorns make sure they're not riding themselves too hard, and remember not to carry the world on their shoulders.

"MY WORK IS GOOD."

"I AM APPRECIATED."

"I CAN SHARE MY BURDENS WITH OTHERS."

4 Things a Capricorn *NEVER wants to hear*

Diligent, responsible Capricorns take a while to warm up to people. Take the relationship too fast, and you're bound to see their walls come up just as fast. This hardworking sign hates mistakes and excuses, so keep your distance and take things slowly, if you want to stay on the sea goat's good side. Also avoid these four phrases.

"Can I tell you something personal?"
"Let's not talk about work."
"I was just joking around."
"You missed a typo."

COLORS
THAT HELP
CAPRICORNS
WORK

Neutral, grounded Capricorns prefer neutral, grounded colors that won't distract their eyes from the prize. Like the other earth signs, they prefer colors that you can see in nature, and that evoke a quiet patch of woods or a sunny cliff by the sea. Capricorns should incorporate these six colors into their workspace if they want to feel transported while they work.

Chocolate Brown

Coffee

Sage Green

Cream or Ivory

Pewter Gray

A Hint of Mauve

5 BOOKS
EVERY CAPRICORN HAS TO READ IN THEIR LIFETIME

When Capricorns open a book, they want to open a tome. They love to take on something hefty, and want to feel like they're bettering themselves with what they read. That's why they tend to gravitate toward the classics. That's why these five books should be on every Capricorn's shelves.

1. *Anna Karenina*—Leo Tolstoy
2. *The Lord of the Rings*—J. R. R. Tolkien
3. *Mrs. Dalloway*—Virginia Woolf
4. *A Brief History of Time*—Stephen Hawking
5. *Alexander Hamilton*—Ron Chernow (One of the inspirations behind fellow Capricorn Lin-Manuel Miranda's hit musical *Hamilton*!)

10 perfect jobs
FOR CAPRICORN

Hardworking, competitive Capricorn wants the opportunity to excel. Any field they enter has to have upward mobility into the stratosphere, with the ability to learn new things and expand their expertise. No dead-end jobs here. Meticulous Capricorns love the opportunity to restore order, and have the work ethic to make amazing things happen. Here are ten career paths where they can do just that.

1. LAWYER
2. MALL COP
3. ECONOMIST
4. ARCHITECT
5. COMPUTER PROGRAMMER
6. ESCAPE ROOM BUILDER
7. SILICON VALLEY BILLIONAIRE
8. JUDGE
9. FOUNDER/CEO
10. VENTURE CAPITALIST

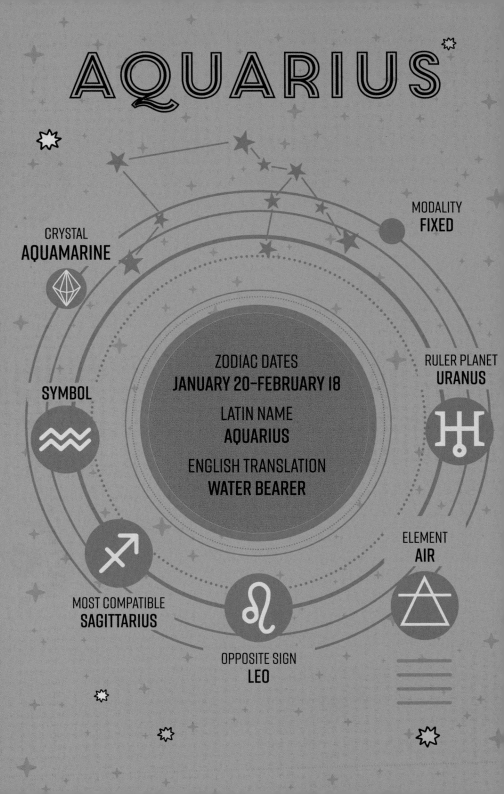

10
PERFECT JOBS
for Aquarius

Aquarians aren't happy unless they're working for the greater good, solving the problems of the world, and giving a voice to the voiceless. That might sound like a tall order, but Aquarians have lofty goals and need to feel connected to a larger purpose to thrive. With these ten jobs, they'll be able to succeed and more.

1. HUMAN RIGHTS LAWYER
2. ASTROLOGER
3. INVENTOR
4. SOCIAL WORKER
5. ALIEN INVESTIGATOR
6. PROFESSOR OF PHILOSOPHY
7. STARVING ARTIST
8. SPEECHWRITER
9. DIPLOMAT
10. MONARCH

5 BOOKS
EVERY AQUARIUS HAS TO READ IN THEIR
lifetime

When Aquarians engage their epic imagination, they want to use it to explore what could be. They want to delve into big ideas, and love heady books that don't follow the rules. These five books ask big questions, play with language, and challenge the status quo. They're perfect for rebellious water bearers.

1. *The Giver*
   —Lois Lowry

2. *Ender's Game*
   —Orson Scott Card

3. *As I Lay Dying*
   —William Faulkner

4. *Thinking, Fast and Slow*
   —Daniel Kahneman

5. *East of Eden*
   —John Steinbeck

AFFIRMATIONS FOR AN AQUARIAN
to live their
best life

Aquarians have big dreams, but need to keep their own power in mind to get things done. They're often flying solo and can be perceived as outsiders, so they'll need to stay focused on their own strengths and tune out the noise if they really want to make a difference. These three affirmations will help.

"I have the power to change the world."

"Good things flow through me."

"I embrace my differences."

COLORS THAT HELP AQUARIANS
FREE THEIR MIND

As an air sign that is represented by the water bearer, blues are incredibly powerful for Aquarians. It's no coincidence that "aqua" is right there in the name. Colors that connect them to the sky above and the sea below will help Aquarians break free from conventional thinking. Keeping these colors handy can help with brainstorming, writing sessions, or any time an Aquarian needs fresh ideas.

1. Aquamarine
2. Turquoise
3. Violet
4. Sky Blue
5. Electric Blue
6. Pure White

5 REASONS
AQUARIUS IS THE BEST FRIEND EVER

Aquarians can be difficult to get close to, as they spend a lot of time thinking about the world at large rather than the people right in front of them. That said, once an Aquarian calls you a friend, you've gained someone who will always respect you and your counsel. Aquarians only befriend people who they find intriguing and whose intellect inspires them, meaning they are friends who like you for you. Here are five other things that Aquarian friends bring to the table.

1. THEY NEVER OVERSTAY THEIR WELCOME.
2. THEY'LL STAND UP FOR YOU.
3. THEY'RE GREAT FOR LATE-NIGHT DEEP DISCUSSIONS.
4. THEY'LL FOLLOW YOU OFF THE BEATEN PATH.
5. THEY LOVE AN ADVENTURE.

4 THINGS AQUARIUS NEVER WANTS TO HEAR

Aquarians think big and play by nobody's rules. So it stands to reason that trying to shrink their dreams or tell them what to do are going to result in the wrath of the water bearer—and you may get wet. Avoid these four attempts at slowing an Aquarian's roll unless you want to end up soaked.

> "That's off limits."
> "Be realistic."
> "You can't."
> "No."

7 SIGNS AN AQUARIAN IS FLIRTING WITH YOU

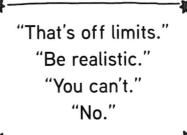

Witty and spontaneous, Aquarians like to grab a potential partner's attention with their intellect (while also subtly testing that yours is up to snuff). They love witty repartee, and find nothing more tantalizing than bantering back and forth for hours. Keep up and keep an eye out for these seven signs, which mean you probably have an Aquarian admirer.

1. They tell you their theory of everything.
2. They lend you a book and ask for your thoughts.
3. They spend all night talking to you.
4. They make a joke only you would understand.
5. They text you an article based on your last conversation.
6. They send you little musings at odd hours.
7. You catch them sketching you from afar.

10 places Aquarius *should live,* even for just a little while

Open-minded Aquarians need to settle somewhere where free expression is encouraged. They gravitate toward peaceful countries known for progressive ideals and forward-thinking people. They love thoughtful, interesting people who aren't afraid to get a little weird. Here are ten places they should settle on their quest for truth.

1. AMSTERDAM, NETHERLANDS
2. SAN FRANCISCO, CALIFORNIA
3. COPENHAGEN, DENMARK
4. HEREDIA, COSTA RICA
5. BERLIN, GERMANY
6. BARCELONA, SPAIN
7. OSLO, NORWAY
8. LISBON, PORTUGAL
9. OSAKA, JAPAN
10. QUEENSTOWN, NEW ZEALAND

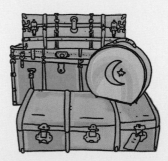

5 WAYS TO AN AQUARIAN'S **HEART**

Quirky Aquarius is not going to be impressed by the usual flowers-and-chocolate routine. This eccentric sign wants to be wooed in a way that recognizes their quirkiness, so leave your usual pickup lines at home. Instead, try radical honesty, oddball suggestions, and showing them you're not afraid to travel off the beaten path or try things a new way. Here are five ways to do just that.

1. Talk politics.

2. Wear something a little weird.

3. Name-drop philosophers.

4. Invite them to a lecture or reading.

5. Give them space.

PISCES

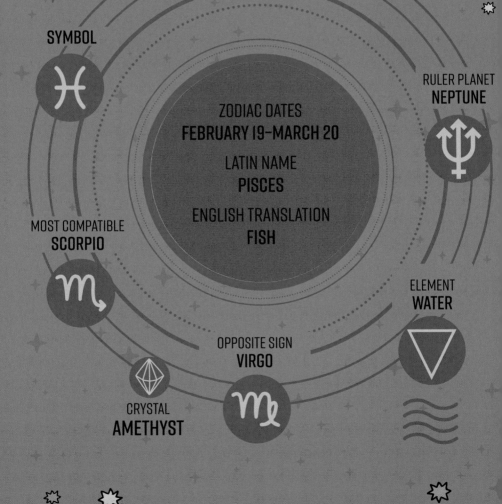

MODALITY
MUTABLE

SYMBOL

RULER PLANET
NEPTUNE

ZODIAC DATES
FEBRUARY 19–MARCH 20

LATIN NAME
PISCES

ENGLISH TRANSLATION
FISH

MOST COMPATIBLE
SCORPIO

ELEMENT
WATER

OPPOSITE SIGN
VIRGO

CRYSTAL
AMETHYST

5 WAYS TO A PISCES'S HEART

Pisces are natural romantics, meaning their heart is always open to love. In order to win a Pisces's heart, they'll want to be romanced. The cheesier the moves, the better. A dozen roses, heart-shaped chocolates, love poems in iambic pentameter are all ways to lay claim to a Pisces's open heart. These five moves won't hurt, either.

1. STAGE THE MEET-CUTE FROM THEIR FAVORITE ROM-COM.
2. SEND THEM A VALENTINE.
3. PUT A HEART NEXT TO THEIR NAME IN YOUR PHONE AND LET THEM SEE.
4. INVITE THEM ON A PICNIC.
5. PAINT THEM.

COLORS THAT HELP PISCES EXPRESS THEIR CREATIVITY

Pisces want colors that help them feel safe and emotionally cared for. Colors that evoke the safety of a nursery will help sensitive Pisces feel comfortable enough to create a necessary part of any happy Pisces's life. Pisces who want a creative boost should add these colors to their sewing corner, writing desk, or crafting table and see what happens.

STERLING SILVER

SEAFOAM GREEN

PEACH

BUTTER YELLOW

LAVENDER

AFFIRMATIONS FOR A PISCES TO live their best life

Ultra-empathetic Pisces can become insecure and confused by all the outside influences they take on. By making other people's emotions their responsibility, Pisces can cloud the connection to their own true feelings. By using these three affirmations, Pisces can learn not to put themselves aside when their gut says to stand firm.

"I protect my energy from outside influence."
"My emotions are valid."
"I honor my intuition."

7
signs A PISCES
is flirting with you

Pisces love to woo and be wooed, and their techniques will come straight from their favorite romance novel. This lovey-dovey sign wears their hearts on their sleeves and can't help but drop hints that they care. If any of these seven signs appear in your relationship with a Pisces, it's safe to say they're in love.

1. They make you a friendship bracelet.
2. They share their most recent heartbreak.
3. They pick a flower and bring it to you.
4. You smile. They blush.
5. They start sending poetry to you.
6. They make you a mix of their favorite songs.
7. They ask you how you're feeling (even though they already know).

5
BOOKS
EVERY PISCES HAS TO READ IN THEIR
lifetime

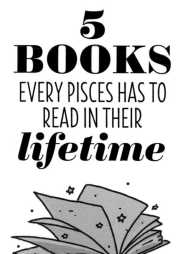

Pisces love magic and fantasy. They want books that will fuel their optimism and provide them with more than a healthy dose of whimsy. Whether the books be literal fantasy or true stories about how optimism can make life worth living, these five books will stay on a Pisces's mind for years to come.

Practical Magic—Alice Hoffman

Love in the Time of Cholera—Gabriel García Márquez (a Pisces!)

A Midsummer Night's Dream—William Shakespeare

An Ideal Husband—Oscar Wilde

Year of Yes—Shonda Rhimes

4 THINGS A PISCES NEVER wants to hear

Sensitive Pisces are used to having their feelings discounted, but that doesn't mean they like it. Try to disconnect a Pisces from their emotions or discount their emotional response, and this animal-loving sign is bound to get miffed. And yes, that does include telling them they can't bring their emotional support pet.

"Stop being so sensitive."

"We're on a tight schedule."

"There's nothing to worry about."

"No dogs allowed."

10 PERFECT JOBS
FOR PISCES

Pisces want their work to feel like play, whether that translates to fame and wealth or not. They want jobs where their creativity is going to be celebrated. And something that doesn't have defined working hours won't hurt, either. Here are ten jobs that will expand a Pisces's life, not confine it.

1. CARICATURE ARTIST
2. POET LAUREATE
3. CHILDREN'S BOOK ILLUSTRATOR
4. CHILDREN'S BOOK AUTHOR
5. TRAVELING MUSICIAN
6. VETERINARIAN
7. BABYSITTER
8. PHOTOGRAPHER
9. MEDIUM
10. DREAM INTERPRETER

5 reasons Pisces are the *best friends* ever

Ultra-empathetic Pisces can be such good friends they sometimes have to make sure they're not taking on too much of their friends' emotions, so can be guarded about who they let dump on them emotionally. Once they let you into their inner circle, though, you'll find a friend whose empathy knows no bounds, and who you can always count on to at least try to understand where you're coming from. Here are five reasons why Pisces make such good friends.

1. Their shoulders are perfect for crying on.

2. They're great listeners.

3. They'll never downplay your emotions.

4. They're not judgmental at all.

5. They always understand how you're feeling.

10 PLACES A PISCES SHOULD LIVE, **even for just a little while**

Pisces are highly creative beings. They want to go to places that value art and, more importantly, the artist's way of life. They want places that value creativity first and work second—even if that means traveling a bit to get to the grocery store or a less-than-reliable mail delivery. Here are ten cities that will satisfy a Pisces's need to live the artist's life.

1. PARIS, FRANCE
2. SÃO PAULO, BRAZIL
3. MEXICO CITY, MEXICO
4. FLORENCE, ITALY
5. LAGOS, NIGERIA
6. BERLIN, GERMANY
7. HAVANA, CUBA
8. BUENOS AIRES, ARGENTINA
9. SAN FRANCISCO, CALIFORNIA
10. BUDAPEST, HUNGARY

THE
STAR SIGNS
COMPARED

CHAPTER 2

The signs
AS FRIENDS

Friendships are some of the most important relationships in a person's life, and each sign brings something different to the friendship table. Here's what you can expect to get from friendships with every sign.

♈	**Aries**	Always thinks up the best adventures.
♉	**Taurus**	Always shares their food.
♊	**Gemini**	Can always talk their way into the VIP room.
♋	**Cancer**	Never comments on your ugly-crying.
♌	**Leo**	The best shopping buddy.
♍	**Virgo**	The one who will tell you like it is.
♎	**Libra**	Introduces you to their friends, who also become your friends.
♏	**Scorpio**	Total. Loyalty.
♐	**Sagittarius**	Always down for a last-minute vacation.
♑	**Capricorn**	Whispers the perfect thing to crack you up.
♒	**Aquarius**	The one who will make you think.
♓	**Pisces**	Knows what you're feeling without saying a word.

HOW EACH SIGN **MAKES** FRIENDS

Everyone has a different strategy for making new friends, and a lot of it has to do with your sign. Notice any of the signs making the following moves, and you've got a new bestie in the making.

♈
Walks right up and introduces themselves.

♉
Judges from afar, then offers food.

♊
Just shows up and smiles.

♋
Finds one person at the party to talk to all night.

♌
Showers you with compliments.

♍
Offers to help organize your closet.

♎
Follows you on all socials immediately.

♏
Offers you a little something from their flask.

♐
Launches into their best story.

♑
Offers to buy the next round.

♒
DMs you the perfect meme.

♓
Invites you to their poetry slam
(and insists you perform).

♈ TELLING THEM WHAT TO DO.

♉ MAKING CHANGES TO THE PLAN.

♊ ASKING FOR A FIRM COMMITMENT.

♋ NOT SAYING "THANK YOU."

♌ NOT NOTICING THEIR NEW HAIRCUT.

♍ NOT PAYING ATTENTION TO DETAILS.

♎ STARTING AN ARGUMENT.

♏ LEAVING THEIR TEXTS ON "READ."

♐ GETTING CAUGHT IN A LIE.

♑ TALKING ABOUT YOURSELF.

♒ BEING IGNORANT OF WORLD EVENTS.

♓ NOT NOTICING WHEN THEY'RE SAD.

THE FASTEST ⚡⚡⚡ WAY TO MAKE EACH SIGN MAD AT YOU

Each sign has a particular set of pet peeves that will set them off, no matter what mood they're in. Here's how you can be sure to get each sign bristling with anger.

What each sign is getting you for
YOUR BIRTHDAY

Each sign has a different way of showing that they care, meaning they all look at gift-giving differently. Here's what you should expect to get from every sign on your next birthday party.

ARIES: *Something they saw on their way to the party.*

TAURUS: *A big bottle of your favorite perfume.*

GEMINI: *A gift card so that you can choose something for yourself.*

CANCER: *A friendship bracelet.*

LEO: *Dinner at their favorite restaurant.*

VIRGO: *Something you had no idea you needed, but they noticed right away.*

LIBRA: *A houseplant.*

SCORPIO: *A gag-based gift that only you two understand.*

SAGITTARIUS: *An elaborate dinner party.*

CAPRICORN: *A new blow-dryer because they remembered you said you needed one.*

AQUARIUS: *A skydiving adventure for two.*

PISCES: *Something they made themselves.*

THE SIGNS ON
MOVIE
night

Everyone loves a movie night! Here's what you can expect when you invite each sign to your movie marathon.

ARIES: *Sulks if their movie choice gets vetoed.*

TAURUS: *Always has the best popcorn hacks.*

GEMINI: *Talks through the whole thing.*

CANCER: *Cries at all the emotional parts.*

LEO: *Knows the names, birthdays, and star signs of all the actors.*

VIRGO: *In charge of shushing.*

LIBRA: *Gets legitimately mad at the bad guy.*

SCORPIO: *Secretly roots for the bad guy.*

SAGITTARIUS: *Says "I've been there!" at every scene.*

CAPRICORN: *Is the only one who's actually paying attention.*

AQUARIUS: *Leads a discussion on the movie's themes as soon as it's over.*

PISCES: *Repeats all the best lines in their own way.*

THE SIGNS'
RESPONSES TO
SOMEONE WHO
HURT
THEIR FRIEND

Every sign has different ways of dealing when a friend has been hurt, from fiercely loyal Scorpio to peace-loving Libra. Here's what you can expect to hear from each sign if you've hurt someone they love.

♈ "I WILL LITERALLY FIGHT YOU."

♉ *IMMEDIATELY CUTS OFF CONTACT*

♊ *TELLS EVERYONE WHAT THEY DID*

♋ "IF YOU HURT MY FRIEND, YOU HURT ME."

♌ "I'M THROWING A PARTY AND YOU CAN'T COME."

♍ "LET ME EXPLAIN EVERYWHERE YOU WENT WRONG..."

♎ "WHY CAN'T EVERYONE JUST GET ALONG?"

♏ *POSTS SOMETHING SHADY ON SOCIAL MEDIA*

♐ *GLARES FROM ACROSS THE ROOM*

♑ "YOU WILL LIVE TO REGRET THIS."

♒ "I'M ABOVE THE DRAMA."

♓ *CRIES EVEN HARDER THAN THEIR FRIEND DID*

THE SIGNS AS TYPES OF
··laughter··

There are so many different types of laughter, and everyone's laugh is unique. All the signs love to express themselves with a laugh, so here's what you can expect to hear, if you manage to make one of them smile.

ARIES: A big, loud "ha!"

TAURUS: A chuckle and a smile.

GEMINI: Giggles on giggles.

CANCER: Deep belly laugh.

LEO: Loud and attention-grabbing laugh.

VIRGO: A simple "heh."

LIBRA: Comes with a clap on the back.

SCORPIO: Silent laugh—it's all in the eyes.

SAGITTARIUS: A loud cackle.

CAPRICORN: A chortle.

AQUARIUS: A big, loud snort.

PISCES: Sing-songy and delightful.

THE SIGNS' MOST
endearing
QUALITIES

Every sign has their own distinct way of making you love them. Here's what you can expect to love about your friendship with each sign.

ARIES:
Their spontaneity.

TAURUS:
Their chill vibes.

GEMINI:
Their ability to talk about anything.

CANCER:
Their empathy.

LEO:
The way they light up a room.

VIRGO:
The way they're always happy to help.

LIBRA:
How they give the best advice.

SCORPIO:
That they're always ready for an adventure.

SAGITTARIUS:
Their humor.

CAPRICORN:
Their loyalty.

AQUARIUS:
The way they let their freak flag fly.

PISCES:
Their open heart.

" THE SIGNS AS ADVICE

♈ "You need to take charge."

♉ "Don't stray from the routine."

♊ "The best decision is not to decide."

♋ "Just cry it out."

♌ "This calls for some retail therapy."

♍ "Make a list of pros and cons."

♎ "Try to see it from their perspective."

♏ "Want me to scare them for you?"

♐ "You know, in French they have a saying..."

♑ "Leave an anonymous note."

♒ "Don't let anyone judge you."

♓ "Have you tried journaling?"

Need advice on a big life moment? Every sign is going to have a slightly different take on how to live your best life. Here's what you can expect from each, if you go to them for advice.

"

THE SIGNS TRYING TO

CHEER YOU UP

One of a friend's most sacred duties is to cheer up a buddy when they're down. Here's how each sign would take on that important task.

★ **ARIES:** An epic motivational speech.

★ **TAURUS:** Wraps you up in their warmest blanket.

★ **GEMINI:** Makes a funny face (or seven).

★ **CANCER:** Grows a third shoulder so you can cry on all three.

★ **LEO:** Takes you out on the town to get your mind off things.

★ **VIRGO:** Helps make a ten-point list for moving forward.

★ **LIBRA:** Tries to help you see both sides.

★ **SCORPIO:** Thinly (or not so thinly) veiled threats toward whoever did you wrong.

★ **SAGITTARIUS:** Recommends the perfect book/movie/album.

★ **CAPRICORN:** Offers concrete help (such as free babysitting or picking up stuff from an ex).

★ **AQUARIUS:** Helps you channel anger into action.

★ **PISCES:** Brings out all their coloring books.

The signs on
social media

So many of our friendships are conducted on social media these days, and everyone uses their page to put their best foot forward. Here's how every sign likes to present themselves to the outside world.

♈
Always posting their latest win.

♉
Can't stop 'gramming their food.

♊
Posts and then deletes.

♋
Isn't afraid of a crying selfie.

♌
Always does an OOTD.

♍
Never misses a chance to say "*you're."

♎
Only posts group pics where everyone looks good.

♏
Rarely posts, only lurks.

♐
Considers themselves a travel influencer.

♑
Has a private account with one photo, rarely ever logs on.

♒
Always raising money for their latest cause.

♓
Can't resist a selfie at golden hour.

The signs as
FICTIONAL BESTIES

Television, film, and literature are all full of iconic friendships. Here are some that represent how each sign relates to their besties, from adventurers to gossip girls.

ARIES: Harry, Ron, and Hermione (*Harry Potter*)

TAURUS: Frodo and Sam (*Lord of the Rings*)

GEMINI: Patsy and Edina (*Absolutely Fabulous*)

CANCER: Woody and Buzz (*Toy Story*)

LEO: Serena van der Woodsen and Blair Waldorf (*Gossip Girl*)

VIRGO: Sherlock and Watson (*Sherlock Holmes*)

LIBRA: Rory Gilmore and Lane Kim (*Gilmore Girls*)

SCORPIO: Thelma and Louise (*Thelma and Louise*)

SAGITTARIUS: Lucy and Ethel (*I Love Lucy*)

CAPRICORN: Meredith and Christina (*Grey's Anatomy*)

AQUARIUS: Bill and Ted (*Bill and Ted's Excellent Adventure*)

PISCES: SpongeBob and Patrick (*SpongeBob Squarepants*)

HOW TO LOSE EACH SIGN'S TRUST

You've made friends with the signs…now you need to keep that friendship going. Here are some sure-fire ways to lose a sign's trust, just as quickly as you gained it.

♈
You don't follow through.

♉
Showing up late.

♊
Ratting them out for gossip.

♋
Not being considerate of their emotions.

♌
Forgetting something important they told you.

♍
Returning the shirt they lent you with stains on it.

♎
Making things awkward in a group.

♏
They sense you're judging them.

♐
Questioning their expertise.

♑
Being too cheerful— they see it as fake.

♒
Dismissing their opinion.

♓
Dismissing their dreams.

The signs at a PARTY

It's party time! Everyone has a different strategy for making the most of their latest fiesta. Here's how every sign handles a night on the town.

ARIES:
IMMEDIATELY TAKES OVER THE DJ BOOTH.

TAURUS:
HANGS OUT BY THE FOOD.

GEMINI:
MEETS EVERYONE, REMEMBERS NO ONE.

CANCER:
DEEP IN CONVERSATION WITH ONE PERSON FOR THE ENTIRE NIGHT.

LEO:
IT'S THEIR PARTY (WHETHER THE GUESTS KNOW IT OR NOT).

VIRGO:
IS DISTURBED AT THE STATE OF THE BATHROOM.

LIBRA:
ENDS UP MEDIATING A FIGHT OUTSIDE.

SCORPIO:
FINDS THE PARTY-WITHIN-THE-PARTY.

SAGITTARIUS:
MAKES SURE EVERYONE'S DRINKS ARE FULL.

CAPRICORN: ALWAYS STAYS TO HELP CLEAN UP.

AQUARIUS:
DISAPPEARS WITHOUT SAYING GOODBYE.

PISCES:
FALLS IN LOVE WITH A STRANGER.

HOW TO *compliment* EACH SIGN

Want to get on a sign's good side? Or maybe you're looking to solidify a friendship? Here's a compliment for every sign that's just bound to make them blush.

Aries: "Thanks for taking the lead on this."

Taurus: "Your home is so cozy!"

Gemini: "I really loved our last conversation."

Cancer: "You're such a good listener."

Leo: "I love your style!"

Virgo: "Wow, your desk is so clean!"

Libra: "You're such a good friend."

Scorpio: "You're crazy and I love it."

Sagittarius: "You always have the best stories."

Capricorn: "Looks like your hard work is paying off."

Aquarius: "You always make me think outside the box."

Pisces: "I love your energy."

EACH SIGN'S ROLE IN THE FRIENDSHIP GROUP

In a friendship group, people tend to play several roles and bring different things to the table. The signs are no different—so here are the roles each sign is most likely to play once they're initiated into your clique.

♈ ARIES: THE LEADER

♉ TAURUS: THE RELIABLE ONE

♊ GEMINI: THE FUN ONE

♋ CANCER: THE SENSITIVE ONE

♌ LEO: THE FASHIONISTA

♍ VIRGO: THE OVERACHIEVER

♎ LIBRA: THE MEDIATOR

♏ SCORPIO: THE TROUBLEMAKER

♐ SAGITTARIUS: THE SMARTASS

♑ CAPRICORN: THE MATURE ONE

♒ AQUARIUS: THE FREE SPIRIT

♓ PISCES: THE DELIGHTFUL WEIRDO

The signs as
TEXTING STYLES

Got a new friend's digits? Now, it's time to start texting. Here's what you can expect once you start chatting with each of the signs.

♈ Lots of LOLs.

♉ Always has the right gif.

♊ OMG, they <3 abbrevs.

♋ Heavy emoji use.

♌ Loves to give a running commentary of their day.

♍ One long paragraph with perfect grammar.

♎ Sends a voice memo, so you can really get their meaning.

♏ Leaves you hanging on read because they love the chaos.

♐ Copies and pastes the same story to five different chats.

♑ One. Word. Responses.

♒ Communicates best via meme.

♓ Text three months later, with no acknowledgment of why.

how each sign
INTRODUCES THEMSELVES

You can't make friends with someone if they don't know who you are. Here's how each of the signs likes to make a first impression.

ARIES: Walks right up and introduces themselves.

TAURUS: Hangs back because they're not sure if you will remember them.

GEMINI: Says "So great to meet you!" (even though you've already met).

CANCER: Big hugs.

LEO: They don't. You should know them already.

VIRGO: Says "You've got dirt on your nose, by the way, did you know?"

LIBRA: Says "I've heard so much about you!" (even if they haven't).

SCORPIO: Makes eye contact from across the room and waits.

SAGITTARIUS: Launches right into a hilarious story.

CAPRICORN: Gives a firm handshake.

AQUARIUS: Immediately asks your opinion on [insert controversial topic].

PISCES: Says "Didn't I already meet you in a dream?"

THE SIGNS AT A
slumber party

It's a Saturday night in elementary school and there's only one thing to do: sleepover! Here's how each of the signs spends their night away at a friend's house.

ARIES:
Has to be in charge of the TV.

TAURUS:
Needs to know about the snack situation.

GEMINI:
Gets everyone to share their secrets.

CANCER:
Calls mom to get picked up early.

LEO:
Can't stop comparing everything to how things are done at their house.

VIRGO:
Wakes up early to help make pancakes.

LIBRA:
Wants to give everyone makeovers.

SCORPIO:
Tells the scariest ghost stories.

SAGITTARIUS:
Says the craziest stuff in their sleep.

CAPRICORN:
Judges everyone for snoring.

AQUARIUS:
Tries to get everyone to sneak out.

PISCES:
Brings their baby blanket from home.

WHY EACH SIGN TEXTS YOU AT 2 A.M.

Buzz! You're fast asleep but suddenly your phone is blowing up with texts. Here's why each of the signs is keeping you up in the middle of the night.

ARIES: Your mutual frenemy ticked them off.

TAURUS: They need your hot chocolate recipe NOW!

GEMINI: They want to gossip.

CANCER: Mom didn't answer.

LEO: They're online shopping and need advice.

VIRGO: They've freaked themselves out watching true crime.

LIBRA: They're inviting you to a picnic in the park.

SCORPIO: They're locked out (again).

SAGITTARIUS: They've remembered an inside joke.

CAPRICORN: They want to go over the plans for tomorrow.

AQUARIUS: They have an idea that will change the world.

PISCES: They had a dream about you and didn't want to forget.

Each sign's PERFECT first date

So, you've got a sign to go out with you, but where do you take them? Here are some perfect first dates guaranteed to woo each sign.

ARIES: An escape room.

TAURUS: A romantic dinner at home.

GEMINI: A party or concert.

CANCER: Dinner and a (romantic) movie.

LEO: Reservations at the hottest place in town.

VIRGO: A day at the museum.

LIBRA: A picnic in the park.

SCORPIO: No plans—just meet up and see where life takes you.

SAGITTARIUS: Hot-air balloon ride.

CAPRICORN: Tickets to a play (good seats only).

AQUARIUS: Dancing, dancing, dancing.

PISCES: People-watching on a park bench.

How each sign Flirts

Want to know if someone is flirting with you? Find out their sign and keep an eye out for any of these signals. If you see it, they're definitely interested.

♈ Kicks things off with the perfect pickup line—they love the chase.

♉ Plays the long game—they're more than happy to wait for what they want.

♊ Always keeps you on your toes.

♋ Sweeps you off your feet with compliments.

♌ Flashes a smile and waits. You'll come over eventually.

♍ Does it feel like a job interview? They're flirting.

♎ Brings a little gift that "made them think of you."

♏ Intense eye contact.

♐ Quotes Shakespeare.

♑ Pokes fun mercilessly.

♒ Asks your theory of everything.

♓ Lots and lots of giggling.

THE SIGNS AS
KISSING
STYLES

Kissing—everyone's got a different technique. And like everything else, that technique is influenced by your sign. Here's how each member of the zodiac likes to lock lips.

ARIES:
Hot and heavy.

TAURUS:
Slow and steady.

GEMINI:
Lots of talking in between.

CANCER:
Warm and wet.

LEO:
Totally uninhibited.

VIRGO:
By the book.

LIBRA:
Long and lingering.

SCORPIO:
Intensely passionate.

SAGITTARIUS:
Totally unpredictable.

CAPRICORN:
Reserved at first, then all in.

AQUARIUS:
Takes your breath away—literally and figuratively.

PISCES:
Wandering—they're not limited to just your lips.

how to tell if a sign is in
L♡VE

You think they're the one, but do they feel the same? Here's what to look for if you want to know whether or not the object of your affection is head over heels.

♈ They let you pick the restaurant for a change.

♉ They make your favorite snack (and don't eat it all themselves).

♊ They post a picture of you on main.

♋ They start following your mom on Instagram.

♌ They talk you up when you're not around.

♍ They take on a chore you're too busy/stressed to do yourself.

♎ They introduce you to their friends.

♏ So. Much. PDA.

♐ They say "I am in love with you."

♑ They let you hold hands in public.

♒ They talk about the future and actually include you in it.

♓ They paint you like one of their French girls.

THE SIGN
CANCELS A DATE BECAUSE...

Just because someone agrees to a date doesn't mean they'll follow through. Here's why each of the signs won't be making it to their dinner-and-a-movie plans, after all.

Aries: It's the same night as their adult softball league.

Taurus: The restaurant wasn't up to snuff.

Gemini: They just weren't feeling it anymore.

Cancer: They sat on their bed and got too comfortable.

Leo: They were having a bad hair day.

Virgo: Their date used the wrong form of "your" in a tweet.

Libra: They got caught up looking at themselves in the mirror.

Scorpio: They never planned on going at all.

Sagittarius: They met someone more interesting on the way there.

Capricorn: Their boss asked them to work late.

Aquarius: They forgot they'd agreed to it in the first place.

Pisces: The vibes were off.

WHO THE SIGNS NEED TO *stop falling for*

When it comes to romance, we all have our patterns, and not all of them are good. Here are the people each of the signs should at least try to stop dating for a little while.

♈ Their boss.

♉ Their ex.

♊ The DJ.

♋ The ones who are a little *too close* to mom.

♌ People exactly like them.

♍ Fixer-uppers.

♎ The hottest person in the room.

♍ Someone who's already in a relationship.

♐ Starving artists.

♑ People who secretly annoy them.

♒ Someone who lives across the globe.

♓ People who exist only in their imagination.

THE SIGNS AS
cheesy pickup lines

Think you're above cheesy pickup lines? Think again. Here's one every sign is definitely keeping in their back pocket. Just in case.

ARIES: *"I'd like to take you to the movies, but they don't let you bring your own snacks."*

TAURUS: *"Feel my sweater—that's marriage material."*

GEMINI: *"Baby, if you were words on a page, you'd be fine print."*

CANCER: *"Do you like blueberries or bananas? I want to know what pancakes to make in the morning."*

LEO: *"Well, here I am. What were your two other wishes?"*

VIRGO: *"Are you a keyboard? Because you're just my type."*

LIBRA: *"Your lips look lonely. Would they like to meet mine?"*

SCORPIO: *"Do you believe in love at first sight or should I walk by again?"*

SAGITTARIUS: *"On a scale from one to America, how free are you tonight?"*

CAPRICORN: *"Are you a pulmonary embolism? Cuz, you're making me breathless."*

AQUARIUS: *"Is your name Google? Because you're everything I'm searching for."*

PISCES: *"I believe in following my dreams—so what's your Instagram?"*

HOW EACH SIGN HANDLES BEING
R E J E C T E D BY A CRUSH

No one likes rejection, but how you handle it can have a lot to do with your sign. Here's how each member of the zodiac is most likely to react when they get turned down for a date.

♈ GETS SUPER MAD FOR LIKE A DAY, THEN MOVES ON.

♉ WALLOWS FOR WEEKS.

♊ IMMEDIATELY MOVES ON TO THE NEXT CRUSH...WHO ALSO HAPPENS TO BE THE OLD CRUSH'S BEST FRIEND.

♋ RUNS TO THE BATHROOM TO CRY.

♌ SPINS IT SO ACTUALLY *THEY* ARE REJECTING *YOU*.

♍ VOWS NEVER TO CRUSH AGAIN.

♎ ROUNDS UP THE BESTIES TO STAGE AN IMMEDIATE WALKOUT.

♏ IMMEDIATELY PLOTS THEIR REVENGE.

♐ WATER OFF A DUCK'S BACK—THEY BARELY CARED IN THE FIRST PLACE.

♑ FINE ON THE OUTSIDE, TOTAL MELTDOWN ON THE INSIDE.

♒ FIRES UP THE GROUP CHAT FOR AN IMMEDIATE TRASH-TALKING SESSION.

♓ BLAMES THEMSELVES AND MOPES.

WHEN THE SIGNS FEEL THEIR

sexiest

Want to feel your absolute sexiest? The answer is in your star sign. Here are the best ways to bring sexy back for every sign.

Aries:
Immediately after winning a game.

Taurus:
Knowing they're wearing fancy underwear.

Gemini:
When they're making people laugh.

Cancer:
At home, in their comfort zone.

Leo:
When they walk in a room and everyone stares.

Virgo:
Immediately after completing their beauty routine.

Libra:
When they're laughing.

Scorpio:
During sex. Duh.

Sagittarius:
When they're telling a great story.

Capricorn:
On vacation, when they can actually relax.

Aquarius:
When they're reading a book in public.

Pisces:
When they're making art.

What the signs will wear on your first date

First date outfits are a major part of the courtship process, and reflect a person's style as well as what they want to convey. Here's how each of the signs handles that vital first impression.

ARIES:
Athleisure—they're ready to run if it doesn't work.

TAURUS:
Subtle basics and a pair of designer shoes.

GEMINI:
Something they bought that day (and will never wear again).

CANCER:
A timeless classic that just screams "date me!"

LEO:
Something super flashy, then says "Oh this old thing?"

VIRGO:
The same thing they wear on every first date, duh.

LIBRA:
Something shiny, and their favorite necklace for luck.

SCORPIO:
Black on black with a dark red lip.

SAGITTARIUS:
Something they got abroad (so they can tell you about their time abroad).

CAPRICORN:
Something freshly pressed so you know they care.

AQUARIUS:
Whatever they were already wearing—they don't change for anyone.

PISCES:
Something whimsical to be swept away in.

THE SIGNS IN THE BEDROOM

So, you've seduced your sign and taken them home. What to expect next? Each sign has different signature moves in the bedroom. Here's what to expect when you get them under the sheets.

♈ Loves dirty talk.

♉ Totally insatiable once they get going.

♊ Will never say no to role play.

♋ All about the foreplay.

♌ Wants their body worshipped.

♍ Loves a couples' shower.

♎ Can't wait to show off their lingerie.

♏ Never afraid to work up a sweat.

♐ Wants the lights on.

♑ Wants the lights off.

♒ Always wants to try that new thing they heard about.

♓ Knows how to give their partner what they want.

EACH SIGN'S
biggest
👍 *turn-on*

Want to make one of the signs go wild? Everyone has a key to get them going. Here's what you need to rev up each sign's engine.

ARIES: BOLDNESS—THEY'RE NOT AFRAID OF A LITTLE DIRTY TALK.

TAURUS: A REALLY WELL-DONE MASSAGE.

GEMINI: WITTY BANTER—YOU'VE GOT TO TURN ON THEIR MIND BEFORE THEIR BODY.

CANCER: CUDDLING BEFORE AND AFTER.

LEO: A LITTLE TEASING GOES A LONG WAY WITH LEO.

VIRGO: SMELLING IMPECCABLE—AND CLEAN.

LIBRA: SEXY UNDERTHINGS.

SCORPIO: A RACY TEXT IN THE MIDDLE OF THE DAY.

SAGITTARIUS: DIRTY TALK IN A FOREIGN LANGUAGE.

CAPRICORN: GETTING ALL DRESSED UP (AND TAKING IT ALL OFF LATER).

AQUARIUS: BEING WILLING TO TRY ANYTHING.

PISCES: A SONG WRITTEN JUST FOR THEM.

EACH SIGN'S

biggest
turnoff

Now you know how to win the signs' affections, it's time to learn how to lose 'em! Here are the quickest ways to make sure you never hear from a sign again.

ARIES: CONTROLLING BEHAVIOR.

TAURUS: IMPATIENCE.

GEMINI: BEING BORING.

CANCER: NOT GETTING ALONG WITH THEIR FAMILY.

LEO: BEING STINGY.

VIRGO: HAVING A MESSY BEDROOM.

LIBRA: BEING RUDE TO THE WAITSTAFF.

SCORPIO: TAKING A JOKE TOO SERIOUSLY.

SAGITTARIUS: MAKING SMALL TALK.

CAPRICORN: INVADING THEIR PERSONAL SPACE.

AQUARIUS: NOT KNOWING ANYTHING ABOUT WORLD EVENTS.

PISCES: TRYING TO RATIONALIZE WHEN THEY'RE TRYING TO DREAM.

The signs when they are SINGLE

We've talked a lot about the signs in a relationship, but what about when they're single? Here's what you can expect from each sign when they're flying solo.

♈ Pursues everyone, settles for no one.

♉ Has a secret dating app profile (for the freaky stuff).

♊ Seduces an entire party at once.

♋ Falls madly in love with a character in a book.

♌ Tells anyone who will listen that they're holding out for [insert celeb].

♍ Thrives.

♎ Starts reconnecting with all their old flames.

♏ Has a different passionate fling every night (and never remembers their names).

♐ Backpacks through Europe—"the one" is out there somewhere.

♑ Posts lonely poetry to their Insta story—then immediately deletes it.

♒ Hangs around the animal shelter for dates.

♓ Conducts a passionate love affair with someone in a dream.

The signs when they've been

dumped

No one enjoys getting dumped, but some signs take it better than others. Here's what to expect if you're about to give one of the signs the boot.

Aries: A temper tantrum followed by a desperate drive to prove their ex wrong.

Taurus: Sleeps with someone else immediately to fill the void.

Gemini: Laughs and pretends they don't care (they do).

Cancer: Cries for a week, then falls in love at a coffee shop.

Leo: Posts a million thirst traps so their ex knows what they're missing.

Virgo: Takes it really well in the moment, then screams into a pillow later.

Libra: Immediately texts the entire squad for support.

Scorpio: Starts plotting their revenge.

Sagittarius: Didn't even realize you were together in the first place.

Capricorn: Turns it all into a dark joke on social media.

Aquarius: Let the trash talking begin…

Pisces: Gets reminded of their ex everywhere and cries.

THE SIGNS WHEN THEY'RE DOING THE DUMPING

What's your strategy for letting someone down easy (or not)? Whatever it is, it probably has a lot to do with your star sign. Here are the strategies every sign is most likely to employ when ending things.

Aries: Blurts it out during a fight and never looks back.

Taurus: Plans for months before actually doing it.

Gemini: Talks themselves out of it five times before going through with it.

Cancer: Cries harder than the person being dumped.

Leo: Totally dramatic in the moment, then moves on immediately.

Virgo: Reads from their pros/cons list.

Libra: Tries to make you dump them first to avoid conflict.

Scorpio: Scorpio? Ending a relationship? They don't do that.

Sagittarius: Asks for "a break," then moves to a new state.

Capricorn: Rips the bandage off, then makes a quick getaway.

Aquarius: *Disappears*

Pisces: Sends a long letter explaining their feelings in detail.

The signs as

Flirty
texts

The art of the flirty text is something every modern dater must master. But with so many strategies to choose from (funny or smooth? Emojis or gifs?), it's no wonder each of the signs takes a different approach. Here's how each member of the zodiac tackles showing interest over text.

♈ *Challenges you on Words with Friends*

♉ "This restaurant looks pretty good…"

♊ "I've been thinking about our last conversation…"

♋ "Netflix and chill?"

♌ "Should I post this?" *Sends thirst trap*

♍ "There's a typo in your latest tweet btw."

♎ *Drops pin* "Oops! Didn't mean to share my location…"

♏ "U up?"

♐ "Wanna get away this weekend?"

♑ "Wanna hear a dark joke…?"

♒ "You've got to read this article…"

♓ "This song made me think of you…"

· ·

Each sign is attracted to different things. Some like the chase, some like you to be open and direct. Here's the way directly into each of the signs' hearts.

THE *quickest* WAY TO EACH SIGN'S *heart*

♈ **Play hard to get**—they love the chase.

♉ **Lots of cuddling**—Taureans love physical touch.

♊ **Great conversation**—Geminis love to talk.

♋ **Talk about your family**—their heart will melt.

♌ **Compliment their style**—they wanted you to notice.

♍ **Flowers and candy**—they're traditional like that.

♎ **Flowers and jewelry**—they love pretty things.

♏ **Don't reveal everything all at once**—they love a mystery.

♐ **Pay attention to their stories**—even if they've told them before.

♑ **Emphasize what you have in common**—they want to feel safe.

♒ **Tell them your plan to change the world**—they'll want to stick around and help.

♓ **Impress their friends**—you won't get anywhere without them.

What the signs put on their dating app profiles

Connections are made and broken online these days. Here's what each sign is putting on their dating app profile, hoping the right person will be intrigued.

ARIES: Lots of action shots (hiking, biking, running, etc...)

TAURUS: Mentions how well they cook. Several times.

GEMINI: Changes their pictures every day, deletes the whole app weekly.

CANCER: Has lots of pictures with mom, and only swipes right on the same.

LEO: Lots of selfies—no bio because the pics should speak for themselves.

VIRGO: Lists exactly what they're looking for and will quiz you on it later.

LIBRA: Lots of group photos—and wants you to have them, too.

SCORPIO: Puts up one photo with bad lighting for an air of mystery.

SAGITTARIUS: Only uses vacation photos.

CAPRICORN: Answers questions with dark humor.

AQUARIUS: Needs to know your political affiliation.

PISCES: Includes at least one painting that you'll need to interpret.

HOW TO MAKE EACH SIGN

SWIPE *right* ☝

Want to attract a particular sign with your dating app profile? Here are the things you should include if you want them to swipe right.

♈ Tons of activities in the bio.

♉ Mention you can cook.

♊ Pictures with pets.

♋ Pictures with mom.

♌ Proof of a great fashion sense.

♍ Profiles that look like you actually put in time and effort.

♎ Professional photos with good lighting—they care about aesthetics.

♍ A bio that makes you seem a little crazy.

♐ Lots of travel pics.

♑ Off-color jokes.

♒ Photos of your volunteering.

♓ Anyone holding a guitar.

THE SIGNS AS
COWORKERS

Coworker relationships can be tough, especially in an office with lots of competing personalities (and zodiac signs). Here's what you can expect from coworkers of every sign, so that you'll never be surprised.

♈ Takes the lead on every project (even if they're not supposed to).

♉ The one you can always count on to do stuff on time.

♊ Has the best ideas, but then never follows through.

♋ Most likely to cry in the bathroom.

♌ Is always pulling a look, even on Zoom.

♍ Most likely to say "per my last email…"

♎ Really thrives in an open-floor plan.

♏ Never misses office happy hour.

♐ Uses every last second of PTO.

♑ Do not disturb.

♒ Works all day, but none of it was their actual job.

♓ Genuinely enjoys "team building" activities.

PASSIVE-AGGRESSIVE
emails for every sign

How do you let someone at work know they've annoyed you without outright telling them? That's what passive-aggressive emails are for. Here's how each of the signs handles a delicate work email.

....

♈ "THIS WAS NOT UP TO STANDARD." Translation: You really effed this up.

♉ "REATTACHED FOR YOUR CONVENIENCE!" Translation: I sent this to you twice already.

♊ "FRIENDLY REMINDER!" Translation: I can already tell you forgot.

♋ "APOLOGIES IF I WAS UNCLEAR!" Translation: But I totally know I wasn't.

♌ "THANKS IN ADVANCE!" Translation: You'd better do this for me.

♍ "GOING FORWARD…" Translation: Let me tell you how work should be done.

♎ "NO PROBLEM :)" Translation: This is actually a huge problem.

♏ "K." Translation: You have awoken my inner rage. Prepare to suffer.

♐ "CORRECT ME IF I'M WRONG…" Translation: You know I know I'm not wrong.

♑ "PER MY LAST EMAIL" Translation: Don't make me repeat myself again.

♒ "ANY UPDATE ON THIS?" Translation: How dare you leave me hanging?

♓ "I THINK THERE'S BEEN A MISCOMMUNICATION." Translation: You're just not getting it.

THE SIGNS AS
BOSSES

Who doesn't want to understand what makes their boss tick? Luckily, their star sign can provide the answer. Here's how each of the signs takes on the responsibilities of being a leader (or delegates them to someone else).

Aries:
In their element, loves to delegate.

Taurus:
Awful at delegating, dying inside.

Gemini:
Has to be reminded they're the boss five times a day.

Cancer:
Wants the office to feel "like a family."

Leo:
Immediately institutes a dress code.

Virgo:
Never misses a mistake. High staff turnover rate.

Libra:
Immediately redecorates the corner office.

Scorpio:
Loves sending cryptic emails.

Sagittarius:
Always on a work trip.

Capricorn:
Still works like they're an intern.

Aquarius:
Is always talking about the "big picture."

Pisces:
Insists on an office meditation room.

WHAT EACH SIGN BRINGS FOR
lunch

Ah, it's everyone's favorite part of the day: lunch! Whether you've prepped a colorful energy bowl or are running out to get fast food, what you bring for lunch says a lot about you. Here's what each sign is most likely to chow down on.

♈ SOMETHING THEY CAN EAT QUICKLY AT THEIR DESK.

♉ LAST NIGHT'S GOURMET LEFTOVERS.

♊ THEY FORGOT TO BRING ONE! AGAIN...

♋ COMFORT FOOD TO HELP THEM MAKE IT THROUGH THE DAY.

♌ TAKEOUT FROM THEIR FAVORITE PLACE NEARBY.

♍ A BENTO BOX WITH ALL THE FOOD GROUPS REPRESENTED.

♎ THE MOST PERFECT-LOOKING SANDWICH.

♏ SOMETHING SMELLY TO CAUSE DRAMA.

♐ A YOGURT GRANOLA BOWL TO KEEP THEM FEELING LIGHT.

♑ PIZZA FROM A PLACE AROUND THE CORNER.

♒ A BIG FANCY SALAD.

♓ FISH TACOS.

THE SIGNS WHEN THEY HAVE AN OFFICE *Crush*

Work crushes...we all get them. But how we handle them is up to us. Here's how each sign behaves when they've got it bad for someone in the office.

Aries: *Always requests their crush for team projects.*

Taurus: *Just so happens to always have extra snacks to share.*

Gemini: *Always tries to make their crush laugh in meetings (even when it's not appropriate).*

Cancer: *Fell in love when they saw a photo of mom on their desk.*

Leo: *Struts by their desk as often as possible.*

Virgo: *Doesn't critique their work all the time.*

Libra: *Follows on social media immediately, so you can see all their non-work outfits.*

Scorpio: *Confesses their love at office happy hour, then never mentions it again.*

Sagittarius: *Keeps suggesting leaving work early to grab a drink.*

Capricorn: *Whispers jokes about the boss all day.*

Aquarius: *Brings them coffee.*

Pisces: *Leaves an unsigned love letter in the break room for them to find.*

Email *sign-offs* for every sign

How one signs off a work email can be very personal. Are you a "cheers" person? Or do you go with "best"? When making decisions of this magnitude, it's best to look to the signs for help.

Aries: "Get back to me soon!"
Taurus: "Respectfully,"
Gemini: "xoxo"
Cancer: "Sincerely,"
Leo: "Always a pleasure,"
Virgo: "Regards,"
Libra: "Have a great day!"
Scorpio: [Their name]
Sagittarius: "Sent from my iPhone"
Capricorn: "Thanks."
Aquarius: "Do or do not, there is no try."
Pisces: "LMK!!!!"

How each sign takes
criticism

Taking criticism in the workplace is a skill we all have to learn, unfortunately. But how does each of the signs handle it? Here's what to prepare for if you have to give one of the signs a talking-to at work.

♈ ARGUES THEIR SIDE IMMEDIATELY.

♉ MAKES THE CHANGE, BUT SECRETLY THINKS THEY KNOW BETTER.

♊ TAKES IT IN THEIR STRIDE—AND FORGETS EVERYTHING IMMEDIATELY.

♋ HOLDS IT TOGETHER, THEN CRIES IN THE BATHROOM.

♌ RESPECTS THE PERSON FOR BEING STRAIGHTFORWARD (EVEN IF THEY'RE DEAD WRONG).

♍ DOESN'T BELIEVE IT. THEY DON'T MESS UP.

♎ ACCEPTS IT, BUT TAKES IT VERY PERSONALLY.

♏ HOLDS THEIR GROUND AND PREPARES FOR A FIGHT.

♐ SEES IT AS ANOTHER LESSON ON THEIR QUEST FOR KNOWLEDGE.

♑ ASKS FOR IT ALL IN WRITING.

♒ TAKES ON BOARD WHAT THEY FIND VALUABLE AND DISCARDS THE REST.

♓ TAKES IT SUPER HARD AND ASSUMES THE CRITICIZER HATES THEM.

THE SIGNS
when they have
AN OFFICE
ENEMY

What's the opposite of an office crush? An office enemy. If you're unlucky enough to have one (or to be someone else's), here's how each of the signs is most likely to deal with the disdain.

ARIES: Considers everything a competition, even if it's just who brews better coffee.
••••••
TAURUS: Totally ignores their nemesis, even if it makes their work harder.
••••••
GEMINI: Constantly slacks their office bestie about how annoyed they are.
••••••
CANCER: Never lets on, but vents in their diary later.
••••••
LEO: Tells them to their face. Regularly.
••••••
VIRGO: Totally ignores their enemy… until it's time to proofread their work.
••••••
LIBRA: Acts so nice the person will never know.
••••••
SCORPIO: Lets it all out in one very awkward morning meeting.
••••••
SAGITTARIUS: Pointedly walks out whenever they enter the break room.
••••••
CAPRICORN: Is perfectly cordial, but their eyes say everything.
••••••
AQUARIUS: Can't help but roll their eyes whenever their enemy speaks.
••••••
PISCES: Stays polite in person, but the put-downs begin as soon as they leave.
••••••

THE SIGNS IN THE OFFICE 🎥 ZOOM

Let's face it…video conferencing is just a part of office life now. So, how do each of the signs cope when virtual meeting time comes? Here are some of their favorite strategies…

♈ Is ready for it to be over as soon as it begins.

♉ Has a snack ready in case this goes long.

♊ Is constantly using the chat feature.

♋ Isn't dressed from the waist down.

♌ Always logs in with full makeup and a ring light.

♍ Has the meeting minutes up in another tab to keep everyone on track.

♎ Always mediates decision-making to move things along.

♏ Camera off. Won't say why.

♐ Always has a different green screen background.

♑ Always mutes and unmutes appropriately.

♒ Never mutes or unmutes appropriately.

♓ Asks a million questions right as the meeting is ending.

WHAT EACH SIGN DOES ON payday

What's the best day of the month? That's easy. It's payday! When the direct deposit hits, all of us handle the influx of cash a little differently. Here's the first thing that every sign does when their latest check comes in.

Aries: Drinks on me! Aries love to buy a round.

Taurus: Buys something fancy they've had their eye on, then saves the rest.

Gemini: Money? What money? (As soon as they get it, it's gone.)

Cancer: Buys a new blanket for the collection.

Leo: Bottle service in the VIP room.

Virgo: Puts it all in the retirement fund.

Libra: A trip to the salon—time for a new 'do.

Scorpio: Straight to the thrift store for an amazing vintage haul.

Sagittarius: Tickets for their next great getaway.

Capricorn: A fancy watch. Something that says "I'm paid well."

Aquarius: A new gadget they've had their eye on.

Pisces: A relaxing massage or a spa day.

Aries: Always has something they need to vent.

Taurus: Quietly eats in the corner, then drops some killer advice.

Gemini: Is somehow always in there. Do they even work?

Cancer: Always there if you need a pep talk.

Leo: Always has a funny story from the weekend.

Virgo: Would honestly prefer everyone to be quiet so they can think.

Libra: Genuinely wants to know about the kids.

THE SIGNS IN THE
break room

Ah, the break room. That sacred space where coworkers unwind, talk crap, and then pretend they weren't talking crap as soon as the boss walks in. Here's how each of the signs handle their time in this favorite office space.

Scorpio: Riles everyone up against the boss.

Sagittarius: Wants to know what everyone's up to this weekend.

Capricorn: Can't stop talking about work, even if they're begged not to.

Aquarius: Is always trying to unionize.

Pisces: Wants to hear everyone's dreams from last night.

WHAT THE SIGNS GET
FIRED
FOR

Uh-oh. Everyone has weaknesses in the workplace, and sometimes those weaknesses reach breaking point. Here's the thing that's most likely to send your sign to the unemployment line.

♈
YELLED AT THE BOSS.

♉
REFUSED TO MAKE THE NECESSARY CHANGES.

♊
TALKS A LOT, WORKS A LITTLE.

♋
CRIED IN MEETINGS TOO MANY TIMES.

♌
CAUGHT ONLINE SHOPPING.

♍
MAKING THE INTERN CRY.

♎
RAN UP DEBT ON THE COMPANY CREDIT CARD.

♏
GOT CAUGHT TWEETING ABOUT THE BOSS.

♐
NOT ABLE TO CONTROL FACIAL EXPRESSIONS IN MEETINGS.

♑
CAUGHT SLEEPING AT THE OFFICE.

♒
TRIED TO START A REVOLUTION.

♓
TAKING DAILY NAPS AT THEIR DESK .

The signs at office
HAPPY HOUR

The day is done and the clock has struck five. There's only one thing left to do—office happy hour! Here's how all the signs conduct themselves during this important workplace ritual.

♈
Immediately buys shots for everyone.

♉
Is way more interested in the bar snacks.

♊
Ends up joining the other office happy hour across the room.

♋
Gets into a really deep convo with a coworker they've never spoken to.

♌
Flirts with the bartender to get free drinks.

♍
Silently judges people for getting too sloppy.

♎
Tries to mediate an in-office dispute.

♏
Tries to start an in-office dispute.

♐
Holds court at a table telling stories.

♑
Arrives late, leaves early.

♒
Tries to get everyone to share their salary details.

♓
Gets karaoke going (even if it's not a karaoke bar).

HOW EACH SIGN
DECORATES
THEIR DESK

Your desk at work is like your home away from home, and how you decorate it says a lot about your personality. Here's how each sign expresses themselves in their cubicle.

♈
Aries: With memorabilia from past accomplishments.

♉
Taurus: With lots of succulents.

♊
Gemini: With lots of colors and trinkets.

♋
Cancer: A cozy blanket around their chair and photos of loved ones.

♌
Leo: Their own headshots—eyes on the prize, baby.

♍
Virgo: Totally organized, with their to-do list prominently displayed.

♎
Libra: Shiny things. Lots of them.

♏
Scorpio: Giant headphones and a sign that says "Don't talk to me."

♐
Sagittarius: Knickknacks from their travels (in the hopes that someone asks about them).

♑
Capricorn: A laptop, a coffee cup, and a lamp. They don't need distractions.

♒
Aquarius: They don't—they're not invested in this place.

♓
Pisces: Their favorite child's macaroni art.

WHY THE SIGNS **are late** *today*

We've all been there. It's time to be at work and yet, you're not there. So, what's the excuse? Let your star sign be your guide.

Aries: They got in a fight on their commute.

Taurus: They worked so late last night they overslept.

Gemini: They met an interesting stranger and just had to stop and chat.

Cancer: They were on the phone with mom and lost track of time.

Leo: Walks straight to their desk with an iced coffee, says nothing.

Virgo: They're not late.

Libra: They were breaking up Aries's fight on their commute.

Scorpio: Because they felt like it.

Sagittarius: They were reading an interesting article they simply had to finish.

Capricorn: Has already sent an email that they will be approximately 5.7 minutes late.

Aquarius: Time? What is time, anyway?

Pisces: Their morning meditation went long.

THE SIGNS WHEN THEY GET A
promotion

Congratulations! The powers that be have seen your hard work and they're rewarding you with a step up in the world. How do you react? Your star sign has the answer.

♈ SHOUTS IT FROM THE ROOFTOPS.

♉ ANOTHER ONE? WELL, IF YOU INSIST...

♊ IMMEDIATELY PLANS THEIR PROMOTION PARTY.

♋ HUGS ALL AROUND.

♌ THEY'RE NOT SURPRISED.

♍ UPDATES LINKEDIN IMMEDIATELY.

♎ BUYS A WHOLE NEW WORK WARDROBE.

♏ TAKES THE CELEBRATION TO THE BEDROOM WITH THEIR LUCKY PARTNER.

♐ A FANCY CELEBRATION DINNER.

♑ IMMEDIATELY STARTS PLANNING FOR THE NEXT ONE.

♒ THINKS UP A MILLION THINGS THEY WANT TO CHANGE.

♓ HAPPY DANCES IN PRIVATE.

The signs' GO-TO EXCUSES

So, you screwed up at work. What do you do? Well, that depends on your star sign. Here are the signs' go-to excuses when they've made a mistake.

- ♈ Aries: **Total denial. It never happened.**
- ♉ Taurus: **Says "Oh I must have missed it in my inbox…"**
- ♊ Gemini: **Immediately launches into a detailed description of their day.**
- ♋ Cancer: **"I had a family emergency."**
- ♌ Leo: **"I was just so busy with other things."**
- ♍ Virgo: **Says "Have you considered I'm actually right?"**
- ♎ Libra: **"I was just trying to find balance."**
- ♏ Scorpio: **No response. Just a long, deep stare.**
- ♐ Sagittarius: **"I was just doing what I thought was best."**
- ♑ Capricorn: **Says "Sorry, I'm just super stressed."**
- ♒ Aquarius: **"I'm just thinking of the big picture…"**
- ♓ Pisces: **"I was trying to think outside the box."**

THE SIGNS AT THE
OFFICE HOLIDAY
✲·PARTY·✲

Bust out the mistletoe! It's office holiday party time, and the signs are ready to let loose. Here's how each of them rings in the new year with their work family.

♈ Shows up in a Santa suit.

♉ Absolutely slays the potluck.

♊ Sneaks in non-work friends.

♋ Tells everyone how much they love them.

♌ Bails out on the Secret Santa.

♍ Can't stop themselves from helping clean up.

♎ Brings presents for everyone (even though it said no gifts).

♏ Spikes the punch.

♐ Finally makes a move on their office crush.

♑ Only talks to the people they already talk to.

♒ Barely makes an appearance.

♓ Tries to get a sing-along going.

Aries: Has their awards prominently displayed (even If they had to print them out themselves).

Taurus: Has the best desk-plant game in the office.

Gemini: Littered with sticky notes from jotting down half-ideas.

Cancer: Has a framed photo of their mom and talks to it sometimes.

Leo: Has found a way to monogram everything—even their stapler.

Virgo: Has a specific space for every pen, so don't you dare think about stealing one.

HOW EACH SIGN
KEEPS THEIR DESK

You can tell a lot about someone by the state of their desk. Whether it's perfectly pristine with color-coordinated documents neatly filed, or a total mess of sticky notes and fidget spinners, everything you need to know is there. Here's what you're likely to see if you stop by each sign's workspace for a chat.

Libra: Redecorates quarterly based on the latest trends.

Scorpio: Looks like a total mess but insists they have a "system."

Sagittarius: Covered in travel souvenirs so they can think about all the places they'd rather be.

Capricorn: Meticulously clean with a drawer full of sanitizing wipes to keep it that way.

Aquarius: Doesn't bother decorating at all—do they even use this thing?

Pisces: Puts affirmations on every surface to keep themselves motivated.

THE SIGNS WHEN A MEETING GOES ON TOO LONG

We've all been there. The calendar invite says the meeting should be over in fifteen minutes, but Jan from accounting still has ten slides left on her PowerPoint presentation. This is how each sign would handle this workplace nightmare.

♈ DEPENDS ON WHETHER OR NOT THEY'RE THE ONES LEADING THE MEETING.

♉ GETS CAUGHT DOZING OFF IN THE CORNER.

♊ LAYS LOW—IT'S THEIR FAULT FOR ASKING TOO MANY QUESTIONS.

♋ CLAPS WHEN IT'S OVER TO TRY AND EASE THE TENSION.

♌ BLOWS OFF STEAM WITH AN ANGRY OUTBURST ABOUT EMAIL ETIQUETTE.

♍ PRETENDS TO HAVE AN IMPORTANT CALL AND LEAVES.

♎ PRETENDS TO BE INTERESTED THE ENTIRE TIME BECAUSE THEY DON'T WANT TO MAKE IT AWKWARD.

♍ TRIES TO START A REVOLT USING ONLY FACIAL EXPRESSIONS.

♐ GOES TO THE BATHROOM AND NEVER COMES BACK.

♑ WALKED OUT THE MOMENT THE MEETING WAS SCHEDULED TO END. THEY DON'T PLAY.

♒ TELLS ANYONE WHO WILL LISTEN ABOUT HOW THEY'RE GOING TO QUIT.

♓ ACTUALLY QUITS.

THE SIGNS AS
Parents

What kind of parent will you be? Your zodiac sign may hold the answer. Here's how each sign can expect to act when they're raising a tiny human.

Libra
Has the house all the kids want to come over to.

Scorpio
Lets the kids watch R-rated movies.

Sagittarius
Sends the kids to camp all summer.

Capricorn
Lives by the family chore wheel.

Aquarius
Takes years to remember a friend's name.

Pisces
Might need a little parenting themselves.

Aries
Shows up to every game (and cheers a little too loud).

Taurus
Can't say no.

Gemini
Is in charge of story time and does all the voices.

Cancer
Always tears up at drop-off.

Leo
Always up for a game of hide-and-seek.

Virgo
Needs to see your report card.

The reputation each sign has...

Whether your family is big or small, biological or chosen, everyone has a role they fall into. Mom's always going to try (and fail) to get a group photo, Aunt Tess is always going to overcook the green beans, and Uncle Dale is always going to be Uncle Dale. Here's how each sign fits into its own family picture.

- ♈ Getting way too angry during charades.
- ♉ Never being the one to cause drama.
- ♊ Always being the one to cause drama.
- ♋ Being grandma's favorite.
- ♌ "Accidentally" keeping the clothes they borrowed.
- ♍ Organizing every vacation.
- ♎ Needing the "perfect" family photo.
- ♏ Being the cousin who gets all the other cousins into trouble.
- ♐ Their spot-on impression of grandpa.
- ♑ Refusing to sit at the kids' table.
- ♒ Telling inappropriate stories at dinner.
- ♓ Being the baby, even if they're not the youngest.

THE SIGNS AS
Siblings

Sibling driving you crazy? Their zodiac sign may be the key to cracking one of the most rewarding and frustrating relationships in a person's life. Don't tell mom!

✳ **ARIES:** Sees everything as a competition.

✳ **TAURUS:** Outshines everyone at gift-giving.

✳ **GEMINI:** Sees themselves as the baby.

✳ **CANCER:** Defends their sibling harder than they'd defend themselves.

✳ **LEO:** Definitely stole your favorite leggings.

✳ **VIRGO:** Always sides with mom and dad.

✳ **LIBRA:** Always mediates arguments at the dinner table.

✳ **SCORPIO:** Knows exactly how to push their sibling's buttons (and does so often).

✳ **SAGITTARIUS:** Never comes home but always sends a postcard.

✳ **CAPRICORN:** Embodies Oldest Child Energy—whether they actually are one or not.

✳ **AQUARIUS:** Loves your quirks and never judges.

✳ **PISCES:** Not afraid to go crying to mom.

The signs in the
holidays

It's the holiday season! Here's how you're most likely to celebrate based on your zodiac sign, from the person who's in it for the gifts to the one who can't stop asking about dinner.

♈
Wants everyone to open their gift first.

♉
Always goes over the dollar limit.

♊
Bought all their gifts that morning.

♋
Bought all their gifts a year ago.

♌
Takes the decorations very seriously.

♍
Insists on saving the gift wrap.

♎
In charge of gift distribution.

♏
Starts dinner table arguments because they can.

♐
Can't resist an impromptu toast.

♑
Gets everyone the same thing.

♒
Loves to shake up family traditions.

♓
Spends all their time with the dog.

The signs at a
wedding

There's no bigger family event than a wedding, and everyone has a different way they like to celebrate. Your zodiac sign may be the key to whether you spend your night on the dance floor or by the buffet.

♈ *Secretly compares everything to their own.*

♉ *Spent hours deciding on the perfect outfit.*

♊ *Makes friends with everyone at their table.*

♋ *Cries the entire time.*

♌ *Somehow makes their way into all the photos.*

♍ *Always manages to snag a centerpiece.*

♎ *Can't stop talking about how they introduced the bride and groom.*

♏ *Gives a raunchy toast.*

♐ *Always at the center of the dance floor.*

♑ *Secretly tries to figure out how much everything cost.*

♒ *Forgot to RSVP.*

♓ *Takes better pictures than the photographer.*

The signs in the family photo

It's family photo time! Are you in the middle, soaking up the spotlight, or sulking at the back, waiting for everything to be over? Your star sign will tell you if someone is more likely to hang back or ham it up.

♈ Insists on matching outfits.

♉ Does the same pose every year.

♊ Is the reason the photo is blurry.

♋ Always hugs the person next to them.

♌ Always stands front and center.

♍ Brings a lint roller and stain stick.

♎ Stands between siblings so they don't fight.

♏ Wears all black, no matter what.

♐ Shows up late every year.

♑ Refuses to smile.

♒ Makes a funny face at the last second.

♓ Tries to play artistic director.

The family fight

each sign is most likely to start

Family arguments are a fact of life. Here's the fight each zodiac sign is most likely to start, especially if they woke up feeling grumpy. Use the information wisely.

ARIES	Flips the Monopoly board over because they lost.
TAURUS	"Why am I the only one who does anything around here?"
GEMINI	"Mom said not to tell you, but..."
CANCER	"I am NOT crying!"
LEO	"Who stole my new pink scarf?"
VIRGO	"I can tell someone's been in my room!"
LIBRA	"I'm just mad that everyone is fighting."
SCORPIO	Lets it slip that Santa isn't real.
SAGITTARIUS	Always acts like a know-it-all.
CAPRICORN	"Stop copying me!"
AQUARIUS	Paints the family dog pink.
PISCES	"You can't just ignore my feelings!"

EACH SIGN'S PERFECT PET

Looking for a four-legged companion? Each star sign connects with animals in a different way. Here's the perfect companion to add to each sign's fur family.

♈ **Aries**
A blue-ribbon show dog.

♉ **Taurus**
A big, fluffy cat.

♊ **Gemini**
A parrot with a big vocabulary.

♋ **Cancer**
A cuddly bunny.

♌ **Leo**
A purse dog that they can carry everywhere.

♍ **Virgo**
One of those fish that cleans its own tank.

♎ **Libra**
A pair of lovebirds.

♏ **Scorpio**
A snake that looks scary but wouldn't hurt a fly.

♐ **Sagittarius**
A pet rock (you can take it anywhere)!

♑ **Capricorn**
A grumpy old cat.

♒ **Aquarius**
The rescue animal that nobody wanted.

♓ **Pisces**
A hedgehog.

Time to hit the road! When a family all piles into the car, everyone takes on a different role determined by their zodiac sign. Here's their road trip attitude, from most to least likely to ask for a million stops to pee.

⫸⫸⫸⫸⫸ *THE SIGNS ON A ROAD TRIP*

ARIES: *Asks "Are we there yet?" at every stop.*

TAURUS: *Has an entire bag just for snacks.*

GEMINI: *Talks the entire time.*

CANCER: *Genuinely wants to play car games.*

LEO: *Sings along to the radio.*

VIRGO: *Won't trust anyone else with the directions.*

LIBRA: *Brings a neck pillow, blanket, and noise-canceling headphones.*

SCORPIO: *Sleeps the entire time.*

SAGITTARIUS: *Enjoys the drive as much as the trip itself.*

CAPRICORN: *Brings an entire library of books.*

AQUARIUS: *Wants to stop at every roadside attraction.*

PISCES: *Must be in control of the music.*

The signs at the
dinner table

From table etiquette to conversation topics, dinner table behavior is determined by a person's zodiac sign.

♈ CAN NEVER WAIT TO START EATING.

♉ FINISHES EVERYTHING ON THEIR PLATE.

♊ TALKS MORE THAN THEY EAT.

♋ REALLY WANTS TO HEAR ABOUT EVERYONE'S DAY.

♌ REALLY WANTS TO TELL EVERYONE ABOUT THEIR DAY.

♍ ACTUALLY KNOWS THE RIGHT FORK TO USE.

♎ ALWAYS OFFERS TO GET PEOPLE SECONDS.

♏ EATS AND LEAVES AS QUICKLY AS POSSIBLE.

♐ PLAYS WITH THEIR FOOD.

♑ ALWAYS STICKS AROUND TO HELP CLEAN UP.

♒ TRIES TO START A PHILOSOPHICAL DISCUSSION.

♓ CAN TELL HOW EVERYONE IS FEELING BEFORE THEY EVEN SIT DOWN.

WHAT EACH SIGN GETS MOM ON Mother's Day

Every sign loves their mother, but how they show that love can differ. Here's how each sign is letting mom know they care on her special day.

♈	Plans a special day for the two of you.
♉	That designer handbag she's always wanted.
♊	A really nice bouquet (that they may have just ordered that morning).
♋	A surprise visit home.
♌	Tickets to their favorite show.
♍	Something she mentioned wanting years ago.
♎	A piece of jewelry.
♏	Something that makes her laugh out loud.
♐	A weekend getaway for two. (Sorry, dad.)
♑	Fixes something around the house.
♒	Forgets on the day, but sends something perfect a week later.
♓	A scrapbook they've been secretly making all year.

THE SIGNS AS grandparents

Kids love their grandparents. Whether they're full of jokes or they overload you with hugs, grandparenting styles are just as determined by star signs as anything else.

♈ Can always keep up at playtime.	♎ Gives the best life advice.
♉ Has the perfect cookie recipe.	♍ Buys you the toy when mom says no.
♊ Surprises you with a trip to Disneyland.	♐ Has the best stories.
♋ Smothers you with hugs and kisses.	♑ Is already planning your future presidency.
♌ Gets a talking-to from mom for spoiling you.	♒ Loves to tease.
♍ Wants to see your report card.	♓ Is always willing to babysit.

THE SIGNS WHEN THEY ARE
MAD
AT A SIBLING

Want to know if your sibling is mad at you? Or do you already know they're mad at you and want to know what to expect? Here's how every sign lets their sibling know they've had enough.

Aries: Blows up easily, then forgets all about it.

Taurus: Is never letting you borrow their stuff again.

Gemini: Teases you about it until mom gets involved.

Cancer: Goes crying to mom.

Leo: Stomps around the house until someone asks why they're mad.

Virgo: Adds it to their journal page of things you've done wrong.

Libra: Gives you the full silent treatment but won't say what's wrong.

Scorpio: Will still be bringing it up ten years later.

Sagittarius: Plans and executes the perfect prank.

Capricorn: Won't stop arguing until their point has been made.

Aquarius: Threatens to run away.

Pisces: Lets it go in the moment, then slips a note under your door in the middle of the night.

THE SIGNS IN THE
FAMILY GROUP CHAT

In a group chat, everyone always has their role to play. This goes double for the family group chat, where our IRL roles tend to get transposed into the digital realm. Here's what each sign is likely to contribute.

♈ Has no regard for time zones.

♉ Responds to every. Single. Message.

♊ Starts a conversation, then disappears.

♋ Reminds everyone when there's a birthday.

♌ Will use any excuse to send a selfie.

♍ Wants to remind everyone to book their flights for the reunion.

♎ Communicates mainly via emojis.

♏ Never replies, but reads everything.

♐ Tries to stir up fights between the cousins.

♑ Muted the thread years ago, but checks in from time to time.

♒ Has an article they want everyone to read.

♓ Is always sending throwback photos.

THE SIGNS BRINGING BACK THEIR
REPORT CARD

It's that time again! Every sign is different in the classroom, and every sign is different when bringing their class report home to mom and dad. It's not as bad as it looks, I swear!

♈ Immediately compares theirs with their sibling's to see who did best.

♉ Always has perfect attendance.

♊ Has an excuse ready for every bad grade.

♋ Gets emotional reading the teacher's comments.

♌ Gets straight As and wants everyone to know about it.

♍ Gets embarrassed when mom makes a big deal of their straight As at the table.

♎ Negotiates with the teacher to get their grades changed.

♏ Report card? What report card? I didn't get a report card...

♐ Keeps "forgetting" it in their locker.

♑ Can't stop ranting about their one bad mark.

♒ Has a speech prepared about the uselessness of "grades."

♓ Includes a handwritten note from their favorite teacher.

THE SIGNS AT A
FAMILY REUNION

Family get-togethers can be equal parts fun and stressful. And it's probably not surprising that the level of fun or stress you feel is related to your zodiac sign. Here's how each sign spends the family reunion, so that they actually have a good time.

♈	Sits at the kids' table because it's more fun.
♉	Is in charge of making the potato salad.
♊	Spends one minute talking to everyone.
♋	Spends one hour talking to Great Aunt Edna.
♌	Treats the event like a fashion show.
♍	Judges everyone's table manners.
♎	Mediates a fight between the cousins.
♏	Starts a fight between the cousins.
♐	Can make even the grumpiest uncle laugh.
♑	Has to be forced into coming.
♒	Spikes the punch to see what happens.
♓	Starts a dance party with grandma.

THE SIGNS ON
VACATION

Your bag is packed and ready to go, so what comes next? Your star sign can help determine how you like to travel—from adventurous hikes to lounging in luxury.

ARIES Has an itinerary, but never follows it.

TAURUS Always stocks up at the duty-free.

GEMINI Immediately makes friends with some locals.

CANCER Insists on a group photo everywhere.

LEO Spends half the time taking selfies.

VIRGO Can be found poolside with a book.

LIBRA Is most excited for the food.

SCORPIO Is always most excited for the nightlife.

SAGITTARIUS Charms the locals, whether they speak the same language or not.

CAPRICORN Has an itinerary and follows it to the letter.

AQUARIUS Forgets to tell anyone they are leaving.

♓ **PISCES** Tries to sneak seashells into their carry-on.

WHAT EACH SIGN'S
SUITCASE
LOOKS LIKE

Can you tell what sign someone is just by looking at them? Maybe not. But you can definitely tell by looking at their suitcase. Here's what each sign is likely to bring with them when they head out of town.

♈ Bursting at the seams from being packed five minutes before they left.

♉ Covered in brand logos so fellow travelers know they're fancy.

♊ Something light and zippy so they can get places quickly.

♋ Something soft they can nap on while they wait.

♌ Suitcase? You mean five suitcases. And a carry-on. Just for hair products.

♍ A perfectly sized carry-on with a built-in phone charger.

♎ Looks pretty but is totally impractical.

♏ Something that says "Don't talk to me when I'm traveling."

♐ Covered with stickers from their travels.

♑ Indestructible, with a lock and waterproofing to account for all possibilities.

♒ A backpack with just the essentials. They'll figure the rest out when they land.

♓ Is carrying at least one stuffed animal.

HOW EACH SIGN
packs a BAG

En route to an exotic locale? The first, last, and most important part of every trip is packing your bag. So, what's your bag-packing style? The zodiac has your answer.

♈ Throws things into a backpack at the last minute.

♉ Packs their entire wardrobe, just in case.

♊ Gives up halfway through.

♋ Sneaks in their favorite teddy bear.

♌ One bag? More like five.

♍ Meticulously folds every item so that it fits perfectly.

♎ Leaves plenty of room for souvenirs.

♏ Throws five black T-shirts in a backpack and sees what happens.

♐ Decides they'll just buy everything when they get there.

♑ Comes prepared for everything— and we mean everything.

♒ Remembers to bring lucky underwear but forgets everything else.

♓ Can't go anywhere without their dream diary.

THE SIGNS WHEN THEIR FLIGHT IS DELAYED

Everything is going fine one second and the next, disaster strikes. Here's how each sign handles finding out their flight won't be leaving as planned.

♈ Blows up at the customer service desk.

♉ Takes the voucher and books a hotel.

♊ Tries to talk their way onto another plane.

♋ Is the first person in line to start crying.

♌ Says, "Do you know who I am!?"

♍ Uses Twitter to put the airline on blast.

♎ Tries to calm the entire gate down.

♏ Tries to lead the entire gate in revolt.

♐ Has memorized the airline's policies and gets everyone a refund.

♑ Spends the entire delay stewing in silence.

♒ Cancels their plans and goes somewhere else.

♓ Is the only person able to maintain their zen.

EACH SIGN AS A
TRAVEL COMPANION

Being a good travel companion requires a sacred bond. So, what should you expect from your next travel buddy? Their star sign holds the key.

ARIES: Takes the lead on everything.

TAURUS: Pays for VIP everything.

GEMINI: Starts a conversation with everyone they meet.

CANCER: Finds all the best restaurants.

LEO: Makes sure everyone gets good photos.

VIRGO: Makes sure everyone has their passport.

LIBRA: Cannot stop talking about the hotel view.

SCORPIO: Stays out late every night (and sleeps in every morning).

SAGITTARIUS: Has Global Entry and expects everyone else to as well.

CAPRICORN: Gets grumpy with jet lag.

AQUARIUS: Disappears at random times.

PISCES: Runs late for everything.

EACH SIGN'S *perfect*
BEACH DRINK

You're lounging with your feet in the sand, but what's the best drink to have in your hand? Let your star sign be your guide when stopping by the beach bar for a drink.

ARIES
Spicy margarita

TAURUS
Bottomless mimosas

GEMINI
Aperol spritz

CANCER
Piña colada

LEO
Glass of rosé

VIRGO
Classic vodka soda

LIBRA
Shots for everyone

SCORPIO
Bloody Mary

SAGITTARIUS
Fruity sangria

CAPRICORN
Tequila sunrise

AQUARIUS
Whatever the bartender recommends

PISCES
Paloma

EACH SIGN'S
dream getaway

Each star sign has a different image in their head when someone says "dream vacation." Here's what the signs would do, if they could plan the vacation of their dreams.

♈	ARIES	*Backpacking through Europe.*
♉	TAURUS	*An all-inclusive resort on a private island.*
♊	GEMINI	*A month living in a new city.*
♋	CANCER	*A month in a cabin with all their friends.*
♌	LEO	*A luxury cruise, hopping from beach to beach.*
♍	VIRGO	*Studying sea turtles in the Galápagos Islands.*
♎	LIBRA	*Museum hopping in an ancient city.*
♏	SCORPIO	*Partying their way around Shanghai.*
♐	SAGITTARIUS	*Solo traveling to a new place.*
♑	CAPRICORN	*Scaling the Great Wall of China.*
♒	AQUARIUS	*Somewhere nobody they know has ever been.*
♓	PISCES	*Following a spirit guide through the rainforest.*

WHAT EACH SIGN IS BRINGING HOME AS A
souvenir

The most important decision at the end of any trip is what you'll bring home to remember it by. Here's what each star sign is most likely to tuck into their carry-on for later.

♈ A rock from the top of a mountain they hiked.

♉ A fancy bottle of locally produced wine.

♊ A book from the museum gift store.

♋ Magnets for their entire family.

♌ A piece of clothing they could never get anywhere else.

♍ Handwritten postcards for everyone.

♎ A charm for their charm bracelet.

♏ Will never say no to a novelty shot glass.

♐ Is just happy to have a new stamp on their passport.

♑ Is happy just bringing home memories. They're free.

♒ A seashell they snuck onto the plane.

♓ Art from a local artist.

where each sign is going on *honeymoon*

A honeymoon is meant to be the perfect romantic vacation for two, and that looks a little different to everyone. Here's how each sign would ideally spend their first trip as a married couple. Now, if they can just get their partner on board…

ARIES: Hiking the Appalachian Trail.
TAURUS: A resort in Bora Bora.
GEMINI: A weekend in Vegas.
CANCER: A chateau in France.
LEO: Beach hopping in Hawaii.
VIRGO: Tasting their way through Tokyo.
LIBRA: Boogying through Barcelona.
SCORPIO: A (haunted) castle in Edinburgh.
SAGITTARIUS: An island neither of you have ever seen.
CAPRICORN: On a Norwegian fjord.
AQUARIUS: A yurt in Yosemite.
PISCES: Sightseeing at Machu Picchu.

EACH SIGN'S *favorite part* OF THE TRIP

Every trip has its highlights. Whether it's the food, the hotel, or the views, your star sign probably has a lot to do with which part of the trip you'll be talking about for weeks after you get home.

ARIES: BEING SOMEWHERE NEW.
TAURUS: THE FOOD.
GEMINI: THE LOCALS.
CANCER: THE PEOPLE THEY WENT ON THE TRIP WITH.
LEO: THE SHOPPING.
VIRGO: CROSSING THINGS OFF THE TRIP TO-DO LIST.
LIBRA: THE VIEWS.
SCORPIO: THE NIGHTLIFE.
SAGITTARIUS: FAVORITE PART? THEY LOVED IT ALL.
CAPRICORN: COMING HOME.
AQUARIUS: EXPANDING THEIR WORLD VIEW.
PISCES: THE ART SCENE.

The signs as TOURISTS

Are you the type of person who looks at a new city through their camera lens? Or are you more concerned with the food? Here's how each sign takes in a place for the first time.

The signs at the
beach

The wind is in your hair, the sand is in your toes, and the sound of the waves is roaring in your ears. So, how will you be spending your beach day? Let your star sign dictate how you spend your time in the sun.

♈ JOINS THE SANDCASTLE CONTEST.

♉ SPRINGS FOR A LUXURY CABANA.

♊ MAKES FRIENDS WITH THE GROUP A BLANKET OVER.

♋ PACKS THE BEST COOLER.

♌ WON'T GO IN THE WATER BECAUSE IT'LL MESS UP THEIR HAIR.

♍ RELAXES WITH THE PERFECT BEACH READ.

♎ IS THERE FOR THE SUNSETS.

♏ IMMEDIATELY RUNS INTO THE WAVES.

♐ JOINS THE NEAREST BEACH PARTY (OR GETS ONE STARTED).

♑ CAN'T STOP ANSWERING WORK EMAILS.

♒ NEVER SAYS NO TO A PADDLEBOARD.

♓ GOES HUNTING FOR SEASHELLS.

ARIES: Throws out the map and goes it alone.

TAURUS: Has reservations at all the best restaurants.

GEMINI: Can't wait to practice their language skills.

CANCER: Spends most of their time at the hotel.

LEO: Takes a million selfies.

VIRGO: Never deviates from the guidebook.

LIBRA: Wants to know where to go out dancing.

SCORPIO: Wants to know where the locals go to have fun.

SAGITTARIUS: Gets lost just so they can ask for directions.

CAPRICORN: Brings a list of museums and visits all of them.

AQUARIUS: Wants to go off the beaten path.

PISCES: Tries to get a picture of everything.

·THE SIGNS ON A·

CAMPING TRIP

You're headed to the great outdoors! Are you glamping, or are you roughing it? How a person relates to nature is directly linked to their star sign. Here's what to think about when planning your next outdoor adventure.

ARIES: Wants to put the tent together themselves.

TAURUS: Takes "glamping" to a new level.

GEMINI: Shows off their knowledge of local plants.

CANCER: Brings the perfect s'more recipe.

LEO: Can't wait to show off their hiking gear.

VIRGO: Has planned for every possible emergency.

LIBRA: Is mostly in it for the stargazing.

SCORPIO: Their favorite part is the bonfire.

SAGITTARIUS: Is in charge of campfire tales.

CAPRICORN: Books a hotel as soon as they get uncomfortable.

AQUARIUS: Gets lost on purpose to test their navigation skills.

PISCES: Doesn't understand why they can't feed the animals.

THE FIRST THING *each sign* wants to do in a new city

The first 24 hours in a new place are often the most exciting. So how are you spending day one of your trip? Each star sign is a little different.

♈ Hits the streets and starts sightseeing.

♉ Visits the hotel spa.

♊ Tries to blend in and pretend they're a local.

♋ Video calls mom to show her everything.

♌ Gets dressed up and starts turning heads.

♍ Cross-references their itinerary with the front desk to make sure they're seeing everything.

♎ Heads to the bar to start meeting people.

♏ Takes a nap so they can party all night.

♐ Checks out the dating apps to see who's interesting (and interested).

♑ Hangs all their clothes in the closet.

♒ Starts exploring ASAP.

♓ Already has tickets to a concert that night.

Where each sign is booking a room

Where you're staying on vacation is almost as important as where you're going. Here's each sign's preference when picking a home-away-from-home.

♈ An apartment in the center of everything.

♉ A luxury resort with all the amenities.

♊ A party hotel with lots of activities.

♋ A cozy bed-and-breakfast with an adorable innkeeper.

♌ Someplace thoroughly Instagrammable.

♍ A five-star suite with impeccable reviews.

♎ A room with a view.

♏ A treehouse hotel off the beaten path.

♐ A hostel full of other travelers.

♑ An historic hotel with old glamour.

♒ An ice hotel they read about online.

♓ A private cabana right on the water.

THE SIGNS WHEN THEY GET BACK

Home

The trip's over and now it's time to unpack and unwind. Here's the first thing each star sign does when they get home.

♈
IMMEDIATELY GOES BACK OUT TO KEEP THE ENERGY GOING.

♉
ORDERS THEIR FAVORITE TAKEOUT.

♊
UNPACKS ONLY HALF THEIR BAG.

♋
CAN'T WAIT TO TELL MOM ABOUT THEIR ADVENTURES.

♌
POSTS A SELFIE FROM EVERY STOP.

♍
UNPACKS EVERYTHING ASAP.

♎
STARTS LOOKING THROUGH TRIP PHOTOS.

♏
TAKES A BUBBLE BATH TO RECHARGE.

♐
STARTS PLANNING THE NEXT TRIP.

♑
STARTS CHECKING WORK EMAILS.

♒
NEEDS A FULL WEEK TO PROCESS IT.

♓
CRIES LOOKING THROUGH PICTURES.

Each sign's
favorite outfit

Everyone has a style that makes them feel most confident. Some signs want to be flashy and attention-grabbing, while others want to feel comfortable and secure. This is what each sign puts on when they want to look and feel their best.

♈	ARIES:	HEAD-TO-TOE ATHLEISURE.
♉	TAURUS:	A BRAND-NAME TRACKSUIT.
♊	GEMINI:	CHANGES DAILY BASED ON VIBES.
♋	CANCER:	A SENTIMENTAL PIECE THEY GOT AS A GIFT.
♌	LEO:	A TOP THEY SAW ON INSTAGRAM THAT MORNING.
♍	VIRGO:	SOMETHING CLASSIC AND MODEST.
♎	LIBRA:	IT'S ALL ABOUT THE JEWELRY.
♏	SCORPIO:	ALL BLACK LIKE AN OLSEN TWIN.
♐	SAGITTARIUS:	NEVER SAYS NO TO A BOLD LIP.
♑	CAPRICORN:	SOMETHING MATURE AND PROFESSIONAL.
♒	AQUARIUS:	ONLY CARES THAT NOBODY ELSE IS WEARING IT.
♓	PISCES:	SOMETHING FLOWY THAT LETS THEM MOVE.

WHAT EACH SIGN HAS ON THEIR
WELCOME MAT

A welcome mat is often the first thing that a guest sees when coming over to your home. So how do you want to present yourself? Each sign takes a different approach.

♈ "Beware of Dog."

♉ "WELCOME." Simple as that.

♊ "HELLO" in cursive.

♋ "Home Sweet Home."

♌ Their own name in bold.

♍ "TAKE OFF YOUR SHOES."

♎ The family crest.

♏ A four-letter word.

♐ "Bienvenue" in fancy script.

♑ "GO AWAY."

♒ A custom pattern.

♓ "Hello Sunshine" with a floral design.

Each sign's *favorite room* in the house

Every room in the house has its own special energy, so it's no surprise that the signs take to them differently. Here's the room or place each sign would spend all day in if they could.

♈ THE HOME GYM.

♉ THEIR (FULLY STOCKED) KITCHEN.

♊ IN THE GAME ROOM, WAITING FOR A CHALLENGE.

♋ THE BEDROOM WHERE THEY SLEEP.

♌ THE BATHROOM, SPECIFICALLY THE MIRROR.

♍ THE HOME OFFICE.

♎ THE LIVING ROOM WHERE PEOPLE GATHER.

♏ THE BEDROOM WHERE THEY DO *OTHER* THINGS...

♐ IN THE DINING ROOM, TELLING STORIES.

♐ IN AN ARMCHAIR IN THE DEN.

♒ THE STUDY/LIBRARY/ WHEREVER THEY KEEP BOOKS.

♓ PREFERS TO HANG OUT IN THE YARD.

The signs when they are home alone

What do the signs do when no one is looking? Here's what each member of the zodiac is most likely doing when they know they're home alone.

♈ Working out with full-on grunting.

♉ Eating ice cream from the carton.

♊ Singing to the houseplants.

♋ Showering with the door open.

♌ Hyping themselves up in the mirror.

♍ Secretly reorganizing the cabinets.

♎ Trying on their roommate's clothes.

♏ Breaking a house rule just because.

♐ Taking "dance like no one is watching" to the next level.

♑ Ranting about their boss to no one.

♒ Blasting a philosophy podcast.

♓ Having full conversations with the dog.

THE SIGNS AS PARTY **HOSTS**

Everyone has a different method for hosting a party, whether they love or loathe doing so. For most, your party-hosting strategy is in the stars.

ARIES:
Is always trying to get a party game started.

TAURUS:
Spends all week working on the menu.

GEMINI:
Threw the whole thing together at last minute.

CANCER:
Keeps gatherings intimate.

LEO:
Throws a total rager.

VIRGO:
Started planning months ago.

LIBRA:
Invites everyone because they can't leave anyone out.

SCORPIO:
Always goes until morning.

SAGITTARIUS:
Is the life of any party, particularly their own.

CAPRICORN:
Puts on an impressive dinner party.

AQUARIUS:
Keeps it casual.

PISCES:
Always makes sure everyone's glass is full.

THE SIGNS AS PARTY **GUESTS**

Being a party host and being a party guest are two completely different things. So how do the signs act when the shoe is on the other foot? Here's your answer.

ARIES:
Tries to get karaoke going.

TAURUS:
Always brings a bottle of wine. Or two.

GEMINI:
Meets a million people, then forgets their names.

CANCER:
Low-key wishes they were at home right now.

LEO:
Secretly still thinks they're the host.

VIRGO:
Arrives first.

LIBRA:
Spends most of the time introducing people.

SCORPIO:
Wants to play spin the bottle.

SAGITTARIUS:
"Accidentally" sets off a firework.

CAPRICORN:
Stands by the food and judges people.

AQUARIUS:
Makes an Irish exit.

PISCES:
Can be found on the dance floor.

THE BEST
houseplant
FOR EACH SIGN

Houseplants are one of the best and easiest ways to bring a little life into your home. And with endless varieties to choose from, each sign has a different reason for gravitating toward a different plant.

ARIES: A striking succulent.

TAURUS: A money tree to increase cash flow.

GEMINI: An adaptable spider plant.

CANCER: A prayer plant that closes up at night.

LEO: An eye-catching giant monstera.

VIRGO: A high-maintenance orchid.

LIBRA: Petite and pretty string of pearls.

SCORPIO: A Venus flytrap to freak out guests.

SAGITTARIUS: A virtually unkillable snake plant.

CAPRICORN: No-nonsense English ivy.

AQUARIUS: An easygoing air plant.

PISCES: A romantic heart-leaf philodendron.

THE SIGNS AS
NEIGHBORS

Neighbor relationships can be as complicated as they are rewarding. How well someone relates to the people with homes on either side of them can often come down to a clash of zodiac signs. Best to come prepared.

ARIES: Gets competitive with the holiday decorations.

TAURUS: Wants everyone to see their fancy car in the driveway.

GEMINI: Is always popping over just to chat.

CANCER: Is always bringing over excess baked goods.

LEO: Throws the best parties.

VIRGO: Isn't afraid to tell someone their lawn is overgrown.

LIBRA: Grows the prettiest flowers in the neighborhood.

SCORPIO: Is only seen at night.

SAGITTARIUS: Is never seen at all.

CAPRICORN: Always lets you borrow their tools.

AQUARIUS: Gets into trouble for their lawn ornaments.

PISCES: Their door is always open.

Each sign's idea of a perfect
morning

Your morning can set the tone for your day and the idea of a "perfect morning" differs from person to person, sign to sign. Here's what each sign means when they say they "had a perfect start to the day."

ARIES: Made it to their morning fitness class.

TAURUS: Ate a balanced breakfast.

GEMINI: Hit the snooze button one more time.

CANCER: Woke up with someone they love.

LEO: Got to do their full beauty routine.

VIRGO: Woke up early to make their to-do list (which was also on their to-do list).

LIBRA: Ran into a friend on their commute.

SCORPIO: Went for a run.

SAGITTARIUS: Met an interesting stranger on the train.

CAPRICORN: Didn't have any work emails.

AQUARIUS: Read a book with breakfast.

PISCES: Set aside time to meditate.

Each sign's idea of a perfect
evening

Each of us has a different idea of the best way to wind down after the day is done. Here's how each sign would ideally spend their evenings before drifting off to dreamland.

ARIES: Put their phone away two hours before bedtime.

TAURUS: Have a glass of wine in their fanciest silk pajamas.

GEMINI: Remember to write in their journal.

CANCER: Have a long phone call with mom.

LEO: Make a gratitude list.

VIRGO: Declutter their living space.

LIBRA: Use their favorite facemask.

SCORPIO: Stay up late reading.

SAGITTARIUS: Sit by the fire and work on their novel.

CAPRICORN: Get to bed before 9 p.m.

AQUARIUS: Watch an interesting movie.

PISCES: Soak in the tub.

WHAT EACH SIGN ALWAYS HAS IN THEIR BAG

What's in your bag? Looking into someone's purse is like looking into their soul. Here's what each of the signs is bound to have in there somewhere.

Aries: Business cards.

Taurus: Plenty of their favorite snacks.

Gemini: A toothbrush in case they stay out all night.

Cancer: A picture of mom.

Leo: A mirror for touch-ups.

Virgo: Hand sanitizer and disinfectant wipes.

Libra: Their favorite red lipstick and a hand mirror.

Scorpio: A deck of tarot cards.

Sagittarius: Their lucky keychain.

Capricorn: Pepper spray and a personal alarm.

Aquarius: A notebook to write down their ideas.

Pisces: Treats for every dog they see.

The signs as old HOLLYWOOD STARS

The stars of Hollywood's Golden Age are some of the most glamorous and iconic celebrities in modern culture. With their various personalities and styles, each one of these fabulous ladies represents a zodiac sign perfectly.

♈
Jean Harlow

♉
Elizabeth Taylor

♊
Joan Crawford

♋
Audrey Hepburn

♌
Marilyn Monroe

♍
Hedy Lamarr

♎
Grace Kelly

♏
Lauren Bacall

♐
Lucille Ball

♑
Katharine Hepburn

♒
Jane Fonda

♓
Greta Garbo

EACH SIGN'S GUILTY PLEASURE

Guilty pleasures—we all have them. What makes us guilty has to do with how we relate to the world and what we find embarrassing, all of which is dictated by a person's star sign.

ARIES: Singing in the shower.
TAURUS: Pancakes for dinner.
GEMINI: Reality television.
CANCER: Eating in bed.
LEO: Online shopping.
VIRGO: Blasting show tunes.
LIBRA: Eating Nutella with their fingers.
SCORPIO: Stalking their exes on social media.
SAGITTARIUS: Writing secret fan fiction.
CAPRICORN: Sleeping in late.
AQUARIUS: Late-night fast food.
PISCES: Dancing in their underwear.

★ ★ ★ ★ ★ ★ ★

THE SIGNS AS
home decorating styles

★ ★ ★ ★ ★ ★ ★

Your home is a reflection of who you are inside, so it should come as no surprise that it's also a reflection of your zodiac sign. Here's the home décor style that will make each sign feel most at home.

ARIES: Rustic yet regal

TAURUS: Practical and comfortable Farmhouse Chic

GEMINI: Colorful, organic Mid-Century Modern

CANCER: Colonial coziness

LEO: Bold maximalism

VIRGO: Clean and simple Scandinavian

LIBRA: Harmonious and Asian-inspired

SCORPIO: An Art Deco throwback

SAGITTARIUS: Art-focused eclectic

CAPRICORN: Classic French countryside

AQUARIUS: Industrial and tech-centered

PISCES: Bohemian Rhapsody

THE SIGNS AFTER A *long day*

We'd all love for our work day to end promptly at 5 p.m., but sometimes the universe has other plans. Here's how each sign blows off steam after an extra-tiring day on the job.

- ♈ Falls asleep with their work clothes on.
- ♉ Eats every snack in the house.
- ♊ Complains loudly to whoever will listen.
- ♋ Grabs their favorite blanket and zones out in front of the TV.
- ♌ Puts on a movie they've seen a thousand times.
- ♍ Writes "Stop offering to do extra work" in their notebook until it sinks in.
- ♎ Writes a scorched-earth email to the boss but doesn't send it.
- ♏ Writes a scorched-earth email to the boss and does send it.
- ♐ Gets in a Twitter fight to blow off steam.
- ♑ Gets grumpy with whoever is closest to them—even the dog.
- ♒ Stretches to Gregorian chants.
- ♓ Takes an extra-long shower.

What each sign brings to the

potluck

It's potluck time! What are you bringing? What someone brings to a potluck is often a reflection of their personality, so it's no surprise each sign has a different take. At least no one is bringing the same thing!

ARIES: Their "world famous" nachos.

TAURUS: A pie that took all day to bake.

GEMINI: Grabbed French fries on the way over.

CANCER: Their mom's lasagna.

LEO: A bottle of champagne—or several.

VIRGO: A giant salad because they knew no one else would bring one.

LIBRA: A cheeseboard that's just dying to be Instagrammed.

SCORPIO: Decadent fudge brownies.

SAGITTARIUS: Homemade Sangria.

CAPRICORN: Showed up early to help the host with their dish.

AQUARIUS: ...we were supposed to bring something?

PISCES: The world's fluffiest mashed potatoes.

THE SIGNS AS LATE-NIGHT

SNACKS

Everyone gets the munchies every once in a while. What tasty treat best represents each zodiac sign? We dare you to try and get through this list without getting hungry.

♈ ARIES: *Flamin' hot Cheetos*

♉ TAURUS: *A big bowl of mac 'n' cheese*

♊ GEMINI: *Gummy bears*

♋ CANCER: *Cookies and milk*

♌ LEO: *Loaded nachos*

♍ VIRGO: *Carrots and hummus*

♎ LIBRA: *A bar of dark chocolate*

♏ SCORPIO: *Jalapeño poppers*

♐ SAGITTARIUS: *A slice of dollar pizza*

♑ CAPRICORN: *A peanut butter and banana sandwich*

♒ AQUARIUS: *A bucket of popcorn*

♓ PISCES: *A Rice Krispies treat*

What each sign is bringing to a desert island

If you could bring one thing with you to a desert island, what would it be? Here's how each sign would answer that age-old question.

ARIES: Several lighters for fire-starting.

TAURUS: Their weighted blanket.

GEMINI: A library of books.

CANCER: A family photo album.

LEO: A mirror, so that they can look good for the rescue.

VIRGO: The emergency bag that they've been prepping for years.

LIBRA: Their jewelry box, so that they can still have pretty things.

SCORPIO: A knife...for hunting.

SAGITTARIUS: A volleyball that they can talk to when they're bored.

CAPRICORN: Spices, so that they can still enjoy some decent cooking.

AQUARIUS: A compass for finding their own way home.

PISCES: Painting supplies.

WHAT EACH SIGN GOES TO JAIL FOR

Uh-oh! You're in the clink. Here's what put each of the signs on the wrong side of the law.

♈
Masterminded a heist.

♉
Caught selling stolen cars.

♊
Gave up state secrets.

♋
Killed for love.

♌
Assumed a false identity.

♍
Hacked their ex's computer.

♎
Stole a priceless painting.

♏
Yelled "Fire!" in a movie theater.

♐
Threw a party in an abandoned house.

♑
Embezzled company funds for years.

♒
Tried to start a revolution.

♓
Caught breaking into the pool after hours.

THE SIGNS AS MODES OF TRANSPORTATION

If you could be a mode of transportation, what would you be? Are you reliable like a train? Or flashy like a sports car? Each zodiac sign answers differently.

♈
A rocket

♉
A cruise ship

♊
An electric scooter

♋
An RV/motor home

♌
A sports car

♍
A train

♎
A gondola

♏
A submarine

♐
A limousine

♑
A local bus

♒
A zeppelin

♓
A sailboat

THE SIGNS AND THEIR DEEP, DARK SECRETS

Everybody's got something to hide. Here's one thing each of the signs would never admit to, even in their journal.

ARIES: They cheat at board games.

TAURUS: Their designer shoes are fake.

GEMINI: They're still in love with their ex.

CANCER: They are Gossip Girl.

LEO: They're not really besties with Beyoncé.

VIRGO: They plagiarized their thesis.

LIBRA: They steal from the mall.

SCORPIO: They are Banksy.

SAGITTARIUS: Most of their stories aren't true.

CAPRICORN: They bury their money in the yard.

AQUARIUS: They're wearing day-old underwear.

PISCES: They write romance novels under a pseudonym.

HOW EACH SIGN MET THEIR

UNTIMELY DEATH

The only sure things in life are death and taxes, and while your zodiac sign doesn't really affect your tax bill (for now), it definitely could affect something even more important: your untimely death. Here's how.

♈ **ARIES:** Scaling the side of a mountain.

♉ **TAURUS:** Choking on a piece of gold leaf.

♊ **GEMINI:** Said the wrong thing to the wrong person.

♋ **CANCER:** Jumped in front of a bullet for someone they love.

♌ **LEO:** Stepped off a cliff while taking a selfie.

♍ **VIRGO:** Forgot to eat because they were so busy working.

♎ **LIBRA:** Poisoned by experimental beauty products.

♏ **SCORPIO:** Joined a fight club.

♐ **SAGITTARIUS:** Made fun of a crime boss.

♑ **CAPRICORN:** In a sample sale stampede.

♒ **AQUARIUS:** Drowned looking for the lost city of Atlantis.

♓ **PISCES:** Got distracted by a butterfly and walked into traffic.

The signs when they see a
GHOST

Do you believe in ghosts? Some star signs are more open to the idea than others, and each reacts differently when faced with contact from the other side. This next list tells you who screams and hides, and who sticks around when faced with a spirit.

♈
Grabs a vacuum and goes full Ghostbusters.

♉
Refuses to move even when the house is haunted.

♊
Isn't surprised because they probably summoned it.

♋
Asks if it can go get their grandma.

♌
Posts a video for all of their followers.

♍
Is convinced the whole thing is a prank.

♎
Can't decide if they're hallucinating or not.

♏
Wants to go with it to the other side.

♐
Tells it to stay still while they video-chat with a friend.

♑
Asks if it needs help with anything.

♒
Has questions about the afterlife.

♓
Is the one at the séance who gets possessed.

THE SIGNS
MAKING CONTACT WITH
AN ALIEN

How would each sign react to a close encounter? No one knows for sure (yet), but here's our best guess as to how each member of the zodiac would greet an extraterrestrial visitor.

♈ ASKS TO BE TAKEN TO THEIR LEADER.

♉ OFFERS IT SOMETHING FROM THE FRIDGE.

♊ WANTS A TOUR OF THE SPACESHIP.

♋ GOES IN FOR A HUG.

♌ TAKES A SELFIE.

♍ CALLS THE AUTHORITIES.

♎ WANTS TO KNOW IF THEY COME IN PEACE.

♏ GETS INTO FIGHTING STANCE. JUST IN CASE.

♐ MAKES A JOKE TO SEE IF THEY UNDERSTAND THE CONCEPT OF HUMOR.

♑ TELLS THEM THEY LOOK SCARIER IN THE MOVIES.

♒ IMMEDIATELY ASKS IF THEY CAN GO TO SPACE WITH THEM.

♓ TRIES TO COMMUNICATE VIA DANCE.

THE SIGNS AS
style icons

What modern-day style icon best represents each zodiac sign's personal style? Use this list as shopping inspo.

♈ ARIES: KATE HUDSON

♉ TAURUS: PARIS HILTON

♊ GEMINI: RIHANNA

♋ CANCER: BLAKE LIVELY

♌ LEO: KIM KARDASHIAN

♍ VIRGO: ZENDAYA

♎ LIBRA: BEYONCÉ

♏ SCORPIO: KRISTEN STEWART

♐ SAGITTARIUS: KATY PERRY

♑ CAPRICORN: EMMA WATSON

♒ AQUARIUS: LADY GAGA

♓ PISCES: ALICIA KEYS

What each sign would be reincarnated as

Do you believe in reincarnation? And if you could come back as anything, what would it be? For each of the signs, the answer is different.

ARIES: A cheetah

TAURUS: A giant panda

GEMINI: A pair of turtledoves

CANCER: A blue whale

LEO: A peacock

VIRGO: An entire ant colony

LIBRA: A swan

SCORPIO: An owl

SAGITTARIUS: A dolphin

CAPRICORN: A bear

AQUARIUS: A narwhal

PISCES: A manatee

WHY THE SIGN
got sent to the principal's office...

Oops! You just landed yourself in the principal's office. It happens to the best of us. Here's the most likely reason each sign has found themselves in detention.

♈
They had a meltdown on the soccer field.

♌
They broke the dress code. Again.

♐
They played a prank on the substitute teacher.

♉
They were snacking under their desk.

♍
They tried to teach the class themselves.

♑
The teacher found their burn book.

♊
They were texting in class.

♎
They were passing notes in class.

♒
They tried to lead a walkout.

♋
They got in a fight with their lab partner.

♏
They snuck into the teachers' lounge.

♓
They snuck their pet into class.

WHAT MADE EACH SIGN GO VIRAL

On the Internet everyone is viral for fifteen minutes. Here's what each sign posted to earn them their brief spell in the spotlight.

ARIES:
Got retweeted by a celebrity.

TAURUS:
Posted a video of their shoe collection.

GEMINI:
Invented a new TikTok dance.

CANCER:
Started an Instagram account for their dog.

LEO:
Started posting outfit-of-the-day videos.

VIRGO:
Posted a time-lapse exploring ancient ruins.

LIBRA:
Started posting their life hacks.

SCORPIO:
Solved a cold case.

SAGITTARIUS:
Pranking the school principal.

CAPRICORN:
Got turned into a meme for their resting b*tch face.

AQUARIUS:
Filmed leading a protest.

PISCES:
A ukulele cover of Taylor Swift's new single.

why the sign left
YOGA
early...

Nama-stay, don't go! Who among us hasn't quietly snuck out of a yoga class before? We all have our reasons, as do the signs! Here's why each of them won't be making it to *Shavasana* this time around.

ARIES: They couldn't get a space in the front.

TAURUS: They were taken out in a stretcher—no unfinished classes here!

GEMINI: The vibes were off.

CANCER: They felt like the teacher was judging their downward dog.

LEO: Somebody was better than them.

VIRGO: The person next to them was doing the moves out of sync.

LIBRA: Their mat seemed dirty.

SCORPIO: The teacher left the lights on.

SAGITTARIUS: They didn't like the music.

CAPRICORN: Somebody farted.

AQUARIUS: They were convinced they knew more than the teacher.

PISCES: They got too emotional during happy baby pose.

what each sign does when they
GET TO THE GYM

You did it! You made it to the gym! A round of applause is in order. Where you head first after swiping into your favorite fitness facility depends on why you went in the first place. What, you thought people only went to the gym to work out?

♈ Competitively lifts weights next to the professionals.

♉ The sauna. Duh.

♊ Whichever machine is closest to the trainer they're crushing on.

♋ Spends most of their time stretching in the locker room.

♌ Gets a spot near the mirror so they can check themselves out.

♍ Thoroughly wipes down the machines before use.

♎ Heads straight to their Pilates class.

♏ Puts on headphones and "don't talk to me" face.

♐ Tries to take over the gym stereo.

♑ Gets flustered and leaves because their favorite machine is taken.

♒ Sneaks into a private fitness class.

♓ Cannonballs into the lap pool.

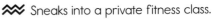

WHAT EACH SIGN ALWAYS HAS IN THEIR GYM BAG

The most important thing you can bring to the gym is yourself (and your inhaler if you need it), but after that it's all up to you. Here are the things each star sign keeps in their gym bag to make the most of their workouts.

ARIES: *A fitness tracker so they can see their heart rate increasing.*

TAURUS: *Fancy toiletries from home—they don't want to use the gym stuff.*

GEMINI: *Several audiobooks to choose from in case they get bored on the treadmill.*

CANCER: *Their favorite fluffy towel because the gym ones are too scratchy.*

LEO: *A change of clothes so no one will see them all sweaty later.*

VIRGO: *Extra wet wipes. You never know.*

LIBRA: *A bag of trail mix from a TikTok recipe.*

SCORPIO: *Extra gloves in case they go too hard on the punching bag again.*

SAGITTARIUS: *A swimsuit in case they decide to use the pool (but never do).*

CAPRICORN: *Their lucky water bottle.*

AQUARIUS: *Running shoes and that's it. The less stuff, the better.*

PISCES: *A secret candy bar.*

WHY EACH SIGN IS
GOING TO THE SPA

Ah, a spa day! The possibilities are endless once you decide to treat yourself. But what brings you to this beacon of rest and relaxation? Each sign has a different answer. Not that anyone actually needs a reason.

♈ THEY NEED TO SWEAT IT OUT IN THE SAUNA.

♉ THEIR MASSEUSE WILL WORRY IF THEY MISS A WEEK.

♊ THEY READ AN ARTICLE THAT SAYS LAP POOLS INCREASE BRAIN FUNCTION.

♋ TO SIT IN THE HOT TUB—THE BUBBLES WILL MELT ALL THEIR STRESS AWAY.

♌ THEY NEED A FACIAL FOR A BIG EVENT.

♍ THEIR PEDICURE GOT CHIPPED.

♎ THEY NEED A FACIAL JUST BECAUSE.

♏ TO LURK IN THE CORNER OF THE STEAM ROOM.

♐ IT REMINDS THEM OF THEIR TRIP TO ICELAND.

♑ TWO WORDS: MUD BATH.

♒ STRAIGHT TO THE COLD POOL TO SHOCK THEIR SYSTEM.

♓ THEY'LL TAKE ANY EXCUSE TO WALK AROUND NAKED.

THE ONE THING EACH SIGN
CAN'T SLEEP WITHOUT

Sleep—we all need it and yet it can sometimes be so difficult to get. Here's what each sign needs to have on their nightstand, or they'll be tossing and turning all night long.

♈
Chamomile tea to help activate sleep mode.

♉
Their 500-thread-count Egyptian cotton sheets and silk pillowcase.

♊
A white noise machine to drown out the late-night thoughts.

♋
Their baby blanket and stuffed animal.

♌
An eye mask for optimal beauty rest.

♍
A completed to-do list for the day ahead.

♎
Completing their 12-step beauty ritual.

♏
Seeing the sun start to rise—they're night owls to the core.

♐
Getting the day's thoughts out in their journal.

♑
The temperature set to 68.5 degrees.

♒
Reading *at least* one chapter of their new book.

♓
Music to help influence their dreams.

How each sign handles
HAVING A COLD

We all know the signs—nose stuffed up, head feels heavy, and a frog has taken up residence in your throat. You can learn a lot about a person by how they act when they're feeling under the weather, from the ones who power through without a word to the ones who need the whole world to know they're suffering.

♈ Insists they're not sick until the last second.

♉ Needs to be served all their meals in bed.

♊ Tells anyone who will listen that they're dying.

♋ Demands mom's chicken soup—even if it has to be flown in.

♌ Documents every sniffle on their social media.

♍ Becomes obsessed with staying hydrated.

♎ Lives in a fluffy robe and slippers.

♏ Refuses to follow the doctor's orders and makes it worse.

♐ Thinks they can will the flu away with mind power.

♑ Takes the day off work but answers emails anyway.

♒ Can't stay in bed for more than two hours.

♓ Uses it as a chance for another rom-com marathon.

THE SIGNS AS
FITNESS CLASSES

Looking to shake up your exercise routine? Let the stars be your guide! Here's how each of the signs are best embodied as fitness classes you might see at your local gym—or if you're an earth sign that you can do in the comfort of your own home.

Aries: A spin class where you can see your speed on the board.

Taurus: A long-distance running group that meets weekly.

Gemini: A dance class that changes themes every week.

Leo: Kickboxing taught by an influencer.

Cancer: A YouTube video you can do at home.

Virgo: Working one-on-one with a personal trainer for optimal results.

Libra: Pilates.

Scorpio: Pole dancing.

Sagittarius: A session on the rock climbing wall.

Capricorn: A 45-minute HIIT class you can do before work.

Aquarius: Goat yoga.

Pisces: A tai chi class for seniors.

EACH SIGN'S
least healthy habit

Just like each sign has naturally healthy habits, each sign has not-so-healthy habits they're always going to struggle to avoid, or to just accept. We can't be perfect all the time. Not even you, Virgo.

♈ OVERDOES IT AT THE GYM AND HURTS THEMSELVES.

♉ THINKS MEALS DON'T COUNT AFTER 10 P.M.

♊ TOO MANY SCREENS BEFORE BED.

♋ ALWAYS GOES FOR THE KING-SIZED CANDY BAR.

♌ PICKS AT THEIR FACE IN THE MIRROR.

♍ IS ON SEVEN CUPS OF COFFEE PER DAY.

♎ NEEDS MULTIPLE ALARMS TO GET UP IN THE MORNING.

♏ CAN'T GET TO BED BEFORE 2 A.M.

♐ IS WAY OVERDUE FOR A DENTIST APPOINTMENT.

♑ ALWAYS SKIPS BREAKFAST.

♒ BITES THEIR NAILS.

♓ NAPS THROUGH IMPORTANT EVENTS.

WHY EACH SIGN
ended up
IN THE HOSPITAL

Ouch. That's gotta hurt. Like it or not, most of us will end up taking a trip to the ER at some point in our lives. Here's how each of the signs ended up needing urgent care.

ARIES: Got a concussion at the work softball game.

TAURUS: Choked on the steak at their favorite restaurant.

GEMINI: Didn't look before crossing the street.

CANCER: Emotional distress from a TV show.

LEO: Twisted an ankle walking in stilettos.

VIRGO: Pulled an all-nighter—five nights in a row.

LIBRA: Tried to stop a fight and ended up in the middle of it.

SCORPIO: Started the fight.

SAGITTARIUS: Got dehydrated from partying.

CAPRICORN: Google convinced them they have bubonic plague.

AQUARIUS: They broke their finger...three weeks ago.

PISCES: Got hypothermia dancing in a rainstorm.

EACH SIGN'S
HEALTHIEST HABIT

Are you a green-juicer? A sunrise yoga devotee? Or maybe you're someone who always gets in their 10k steps per day. These are the healthy habits that come naturally to each sign so they can stay happy and whole.

♈ ALWAYS GETS THEIR 30 MINUTES OF DAILY EXERCISE.

♉ NEVER MISSES BREAKFAST.

♊ DOES LOGIC PUZZLES IN THEIR SPARE TIME.

♋ ALWAYS GETS THE RECOMMENDED EIGHT HOURS OF SLEEP.

♌ NEVER MISSES A TRIP TO THE DENTIST.

♍ HAS A MORNING ROUTINE AND STICKS TO IT.

♎ NEVER FORGETS TO WASH THEIR FACE BEFORE GOING TO BED.

♏ CAN COOK UP AN AMAZING VEGGIE STIR-FRY.

♐ LOVES TAKING A WALK TO THINK.

♑ DRINKS EIGHT GLASSES OF WATER PER DAY.

♒ GENUINELY ENJOYS SALADS.

♓ NEVER MISSES AN OPPORTUNITY TO STRETCH.

EACH SIGN FEELS THE
most beautiful
WHEN...

Every person is beautiful, which means every sign is beautiful. We all have different things that make us feel like we are at our most beautiful, inside and out. This is when the signs feel their best.

ARIES: They're taking charge.

TAURUS: They're in their own home.

GEMINI: They're at the center of a crowd.

CANCER: They're surrounded by loved ones.

LEO: They're in front of a camera.

VIRGO: They're just out of the shower.

LIBRA: They have on their favorite lipstick.

SCORPIO: They're dressed in black.

SAGITTARIUS: They're in a new place.

CAPRICORN: They're in a familiar place.

AQUARIUS: They're talking about their ideas.

PISCES: They're expressing their creativity.

A self-care item each sign would splurge on

"Self-care" is the buzzword of the day, but each sign defines that term differently when it comes to whether or not to splurge on their "self-care" pursuit. One sign's outrageously expensive eye cream is another sign's personal care necessity, after all!

ARIES: *Fancy candles for every room in the house.*

TAURUS: *They splurge on everything, so this question is irrelevant.*

GEMINI: *A vegan leather notebook with extra-thick pages.*

CANCER: *Scented bath bombs that turn into a flower in the tub.*

LEO: *Shoes totally count as self-care. Ask Carrie Bradshaw.*

VIRGO: *The latest super-high-powered vacuum cleaner.*

LIBRA: *A high-end face cream their favorite celeb used on Instagram.*

SCORPIO: *Tickets to the hottest event in town.*

SAGITTARIUS: *Dessert at their favorite restaurant.*

CAPRICORN: *A massage chair they can sit in after a long day.*

AQUARIUS: *Crystals for their full moon meditation ritual.*

PISCES: *Art supplies for their latest craft project.*

THE THING EACH SIGN **HATES** THAT EVERYONE ELSE **LOVES**

We've all been there—it seems like the whole world is obsessed with something, and you just can't get on board. Here's something most people love that they just can't get on board with.

Aries	*The Lord of the Rings*—too long!
Taurus	Cauliflower everything. They want the real flavor!
Gemini	Using Twitter.
Cancer	Escape rooms—they literally want out.
Leo	Listening to podcasts.
Virgo	Fantasy series. No dragons please!
Libra	Superhero movies. Too much fighting.
Scorpio	Musicals. Bleh.
Sagittarius	Baby Yoda memes...
Capricorn	Dating shows. There's no way these people actually like each other.
Aquarius	The *Real Housewives* of Anything.
Pisces	TikTok dances—they want to make up their own moves.

THE SIGNS AS POP STARS

Each pop star exudes their own special something that helps them connect with fans and their audience at large. It also helps connect them to a sign. Here's a pop star that best represents each member of the zodiac.

♈
Janet Jackson

♉
Miley Cyrus

♊
Madonna

♋
Britney Spears

♌
Lady Gaga

♍
Beyoncé

♎
Lizzo

♏
Billie Eilish

♐
Taylor Swift

♑
Adele

♒
Prince

♓
Ariana Grande

♈ THEIR LOCAL SPORTS TEAM.

♉ THE PERFECT WAY TO POACH AN EGG.

♊ SOMETHING THEY JUST LEARNED ABOUT YESTERDAY.

♋ THEIR SIBLING'S SIGNIFICANT OTHER.

♌ FASHION CHOICES.

♍ LITERALLY EVERYTHING.

♎ INTERIOR DESIGN.

♏ HOW TO MIX A PERFECT COCKTAIL.

♐ TRAVEL ETIQUETTE.

♑ EVERYDAY ETIQUETTE.

♒ ALL OF THE TOP HEADLINES.

♓ WHY THEIR HIGH SCHOOL BAND COULD HAVE MADE IT.

EACH SIGN HAS VERY STRONG OPINIONS ON...

Opinions are like...well, you know. That is to say, everyone's got 'em. And some are stronger than others. These are the topics most likely to get each of the signs carrying on...and on... and on...

THE SIGNS AS
PROTAGONISTS

Whether they're an action hero, *femme fatale*, or kid next door, movie protagonists always have something audiences can relate to. Here are a few that will have each of the signs yelling "That's me!" as soon as they appear on screen.

ARIES: *Katniss Everdeen*

TAURUS: *Wendy Darling*

GEMINI: *Alice*

CANCER: *Dorothy Gale*

LEO: *Scarlett O'Hara*

VIRGO: *Sherlock Holmes*

LIBRA: *Mary Poppins*

SCORPIO: *James Bond*

SAGITTARIUS: *Elizabeth Bennet*

CAPRICORN: *Atticus Finch*

AQUARIUS: *Robin Hood*

PISCES: *Jo March*

What each sign nerds out over...

In the modern era, everyone stans something a little bit. With so many books, movies, and TV shows out there for us to consume, it's hard not to become a superfan of something. Here's the fandom each sign can't help but join…

♈ *Game of Thrones*—don't get them started on the ending.

♉ *Harry Potter*—they're a Hufflepuff!

♊ *The Lord of the Rings*—and yes, they do speak Elvish.

♋ *Twilight*—it won their heart, just like Edward won Bella's.

♌ *Pop stars*—they just joined the BTS Army.

♍ *True crime*—they know they can solve the case!

♎ *Friends*—they watch it over and over again.

♏ *Dungeons and Dragons*—they're a level six druid!

♐ *The Office*—they can quote every episode.

♑ *Star Wars*—the original fandom!

♒ Only ask if you want to hear about some very obscure anime.

♓ *My Little Pony*—their collection of ponies is perfectly organized by color.

THE SIGNS AS BROADWAY MUSICALS

As any musical lover will tell you, there's one out there for everyone. Here's a musical that is bound to get the toes tapping for each of the zodiac signs.

ARIES: *The Music Man*

TAURUS: *Chicago*

GEMINI: *Mamma Mia!*

CANCER: *Wicked*

LEO: *Beauty and the Beast*

VIRGO: *Les Misérables*

LIBRA: *My Fair Lady*

SCORPIO: *The Little Shop of Horrors*

SAGITTARIUS: *The Producers*

CAPRICORN: *The Phantom of the Opera*

AQUARIUS: *Hamilton*

PISCES: *Cats*

THE TV SHOW EACH SIGN HAS WATCHED A MILLION TIMES

Everyone has a show that lives at the top of their binge-watch list, even if they've already seen every episode. Put on any episode of one of these shows if you want to get the signs quoting from memory.

♈ GAME OF THRONES

♉ SURVIVOR

♊ THE SIMPSONS

♋ GREY'S ANATOMY

♌ GOSSIP GIRL

♍ DOCTOR WHO

♎ FRIENDS

♏ TWIN PEAKS

♐ THE OFFICE

♑ SEINFELD

♒ THE X-FILES

♓ THE JOY OF PAINTING

THE SIGNS AS
SHAKESPEARE
CHARACTERS

Shakespeare gave us some of literature's most iconic characters, many of whom are archetypes through which we still see people and personalities today. Here's which famous Shakespearean invention best represents each of the signs.

♈ ARIES: **Macbeth**

♉ TAURUS: **Rosalind**

♊ GEMINI: **Viola**

♋ CANCER: **Juliet**

♌ LEO: **Cleopatra**

♍ VIRGO: **Lady Macbeth**

♎ LIBRA: **Queen Titania**

♏ SCORPIO: **Hamlet**

♐ SAGITTARIUS: **Puck**

♑ CAPRICORN: **Beatrice**

♒ AQUARIUS: **Prospero**

♓ PISCES: **The Three Witches**

what is on each sign's bookshelf...

The most intimate part of a person's home? Their bookshelf. A bookshelf represents a person's values and interests, and you can learn a lot about a person just by perusing their book collection.

Aries:
Inspiring biographies.

Taurus:
"How To..." guides for literally everything.

Gemini:
At least one book from every genre.

Cancer:
Their favorite books from childhood.

Leo:
Thrillers that have been made into movies.

Virgo:
Perfectly alphabetized fiction.

Libra:
Books with beautiful cover art.

Scorpio:
Stephen King.

Sagittarius:
Travel guides.

Capricorn:
Perfectly alphabetized nonfiction.

Aquarius:
Totally disorganized nonfiction.

Pisces:
Romance novels.

THE SIGNS AS FAMOUS WRITERS

Have a favorite writer? Maybe the reason you love them so much is because they remind you ever so slightly of your own zodiac sign. Just don't try to hand over that analysis in English class.

ARIES: Maya Angelou

TAURUS: Charlotte Brontë

GEMINI: Jane Austen

CANCER: Toni Morrison

LEO: Oscar Wilde

VIRGO: C.S. Lewis

LIBRA: F. Scott Fitzgerald

SCORPIO: George Orwell

SAGITTARIUS: Mark Twain

CAPRICORN: Emily Dickinson

AQUARIUS: James Joyce

PISCES: Roald Dahl

WHAT TYPE OF
PODCAST
EACH SIGN IS LISTENING TO

With so many podcasts hitting the airwaves every day, listeners can tailor their pod playlists to their exact interests. Here's what each sign is most likely to be listening to while going about their day.

♈ Oprah's Super Soul Sunday.

♉ A cooking podcast (to listen to while cooking).

♊ Deep dives into complex topics.

♋ Two besties just chatting.

♌ Celebrity gossip and pop culture.

♍ Life hacks from their favorite influencer.

♎ An advice podcast (even though they think their advice would be better).

♏ Unsolved mysteries.

♐ Something hosted by their favorite comedian.

♑ A history podcast so they can fill up on interesting facts.

♒ A news podcast they can debate through the phone.

♓ A narrative podcast meant for children.

The signs as
ICONIC VILLAINS

We know them, we hate them, we love to hate them. Here's how each sign matches up to some of the most iconic villains in film and literature.

ARIES: CAPTAIN HOOK

TAURUS: LORD VOLDEMORT

GEMINI: DR. JEKYLL AND MR. HYDE

CANCER: MOTHER GOTHEL

LEO: CRUELLA DE VIL

VIRGO: MALEFICENT

LIBRA: THE WHITE WITCH

SCORPIO: COUNT DRACULA

SAGITTARIUS: REGINA GEORGE

CAPRICORN: DARTH VADER

AQUARIUS: THE JOKER

PISCES: THE SHARK FROM JAWS

INDEX

A

accommodation 131
advice 90
affirmations 17, 22, 29,
   34, 40, 45, 52, 57, 62,
   70, 75, 80
aliens 143
anger 122
Aquarius 72–7
Aries 12–17
arts & culture 152–7

B

bags 137
beaches 129
beauty 151
bedroom, signs in the 101
birthdays 87
books 16, 23, 29, 35, 41,
   46, 53, 57, 64, 71, 74,
   81, 156
bosses 107
break rooms 111

C

camping trips 130
Cancer 30–5
Capricorn 66–71
chats, group 122
cheering friends up 90
city breaks 130
clothes 100, 132
colds 148
colors 17, 22, 29, 34, 41,
   45, 52, 57, 62, 70, 75,
   80
companions, travel 126
compliments 93

coworkers 106
criticism 109
crushes 99, 108

D

dating 96, 98, 100, 105
days, long 139
death, untimely 142
decorating styles 138
desert islands 140
desks 112, 115
detention 145
drinks, beach 126
dumped signs 103

E

emails 106, 108
endearing qualities 89
enemies 109
evenings 136
excuses 114

F

family 116–23
fictional friends 91
fights, family 119
fired from work 111
fitness classes 149
flirting 14, 20, 27, 33, 38,
   45, 51, 59, 65, 69, 76,
   81, 96, 104
flying 125
food 139, 140
friends 15, 21, 27, 32, 38,
   47, 53, 56, 63, 69, 75,
   83, 86–95
fun 140–5

G

Gemini 24–9
getaways, dream 127
ghosts 143
grandparents 121
guilty pleasures 138
gyms 146, 147

H

habits 149, 150
happy hour 112
health & wellness 146–51
heart, route to the 104
holidays 117
Hollywood stars 137
home alone 133
honeymoons 128
hospital visits 150
houseplants 135
hurt responses 88

I

introductions 94

J

jail 141
jobs 16, 23, 28, 35, 40,
   47, 50, 56, 62, 71, 74,
   82, 106–15

K

kissing 97

L

lateness 113
laughter 89
Leo 36–41